SpringerBriefs in Computer Science

Series Editors
Stan Zdonik
Peng Ning
Shashi Shekhar
Jonathan Katz
Xindong Wu
Lakhmi C. Jain
David Padua
Xuemin Shen
Borko Furht
V.S. Subrahmanian
Martial Hebert
Katsushi Ikeuchi
Bruno Siciliano

For further volumes:
http://www.springer.com/series/10028

Jiannong Cao • Chisheng Zhang

Seamless and Secure Communications over Heterogeneous Wireless Networks

 Springer

Jiannong Cao
Department of Computing
Hong Kong Polytechnic University
Kowloon, Hong Kong SAR

Chisheng Zhang
Department of Computing
Hong Kong Polytechnic University
Kowloon, Hong Kong SAR

ISSN 2191-5768   ISSN 2191-5776 (electronic)
ISBN 978-1-4939-0415-0   ISBN 978-1-4939-0416-7 (eBook)
DOI 10.1007/978-1-4939-0416-7
Springer New York Heidelberg Dordrecht London

Library of Congress Control Number: 2014930153

Printed on acid-free paper

Springer is part of Springer Science+Business Media (www.springer.com)

Preface

The Motivation for This Book

The past decade has witnessed the emergence of mobile Internet applications for diverse mobile devices, ranging from text-based office assistant utilities to multimedia-based online entertainment. The potential impact of heterogeneous wireless networks has been confirmed by an ever-increasing amount of mobile Internet traffic, which cannot solely be absorbed by cellular data communication networks, such as 3G networks. For example, more and more mobile telecommunication operators, including AT&T, Verizon Wireless, Vodafone, Orange, T-Mobile and China Mobile, are willing to deploy millions of Wi-Fi access points in urban areas to offload mobile Internet traffic from cellular networks. However, different from mature seamless roaming technologies of voice and data services in cellular networks, handover technologies in heterogeneous wireless networks still encounter many challenges, from both technical and administrative standpoints.

The main motivation for offering this book stems from the observation that, at present there is no comprehensive source of information about seamless and secure roaming over heterogeneous wireless networks. In addition to providing the latest information in this area, we also include recent research results and implementation details from two related projects, which we conducted from April 2007 to August 2011. Both projects were supported by the Hong Kong Innovation and Technology Fund. We believe there is value in bringing basic theoretical concepts and practical implementation together, which can facilitate a deep understanding of the entire area.

What This Book Is About

This book provides comprehensive coverage and detailed insights into the emerging area of seamless and secure roaming in heterogeneous wireless networks, which aims at a better user experience and security guarantees in different handover scenarios. It helps the reader to understand the specifics in designing seamless and secure roaming protocols and applications, while introducing a solid set of general approaches, practical methods, and implementation concepts. Therefore, it can be seen as a textbook as well as a practical guide for the reader:

- To learn about mainstream technologies of heterogeneous wireless networks, and the different interworking approaches to achieving interoperation in different networks
- To understand the state-of-the-art technologies in seamless roaming over heterogeneous wireless networks, and the experiences and lessons from our practice in implementing the **HAWK** project
- To understand state-of-the-art technologies in secure enhancement on seamless roaming over heterogeneous wireless networks, and some experiences and lessons from our practice in implementing the **SHAWK** project

How This Book Is Organized

This book is divided into five chapters.

Chapter 1: Introduction. In this chapter, we will introduce the requirements for seamless and secure roaming in heterogeneous wireless networks, which are followed by the challenging issues in developing the relevant technologies.

Chapter 2: Wireless Technologies in Heterogeneous Wireless Networks. This chapter reviews related wireless communication and interworking technologies involved in heterogeneous wireless networks.

Chapter 3: Seamless Roaming over Heterogeneous Wireless Networks. First, we summarize the related work on handover management and mobility management in heterogeneous wireless networks. Then we describe some case studies of seamless roaming systems in our **HAWK** projects. The main objective of the **HAWK** project is to study and develop practical techniques and mechanisms for realizing seamless communication and mobility when mobile clients roam among advanced heterogeneous wireless networks.

Chapter 4: Secure Enhancement on Seamless Roaming. This chapter provides a solid set of security technologies and mechanisms for implementing the identified security requirements of seamless roaming over heterogeneous wireless networks. It also describes the implementation details of our **SHAWK** projects, whose main objective is to develop solutions to key security problems in providing ubiquitous and seamless Internet access over heterogeneous wireless networks.

Chapter 5: Summary. We will draw a conclusion for the whole book in the final chapter.

Kowloon, Hong Kong   Jiannong Cao
                                                                                                   Chisheng Zhang

Acknowledgements

The authors are deeply grateful to the research staff and students in our research group for their hard work in carrying out the **HAWK** and **SHAWK** projects and their support in our writing of this book. We would like to thank our project group members, including Prof. Chuda Liu, Prof. Weigang Wu, Prof. Kun Xie, Dr. Jun Zhang, Dr. Jigan Wen, Dr. Wei Feng, Dr. Hongjian Li, Dr. Yao Yu, Dr. Xuedan Zhang, Mr. Gang Yao, Mr. Xin Xiao, Mr. Yang Zou, Mr. Yueming Deng, Mr. Liang Yang, Mr. Haitao Chen, Ms. Jie Zhou, Ms. Miao Xiong, Ms. Xuan Liu, Mr. Nengqiang He and Mr. Ye Yan for their hard work in the research projects. We would also like to express our thanks to Prof. Bin Xiao of Hong Kong Polytechnic University and Prof. Jun Zhang of Sun Yat-Sen University for their invaluable advice throughout this research. Thanks are also due to our colleagues, Dr. Xuefeng Liu and Mr. Florian Klingler, who read the draft of the book, and provided many detailed suggestions and comments. The financial support from the Innovation and Technology Fund (ITF GHP/049/06 and GHP/036/08) of the government of Hong Kong Special Administrative Region is greatly appreciated.

Contents

List of Figures

List of Tables

Chapter 1
Introduction

One of the key features in future heterogeneous wireless networks is to always provide the best network connectivity and data services to mobile users through different available wireless access networks, where different interworking scenarios appear during users' handover and roaming procedures. Nowadays, mobile operators have to deploy multiple wireless access networks with different technologies to meet increasing mobility and bandwidth requirements. Handovers between these technologies have to be transparent to end users, to allow a simplified and seamless on-the-move roaming experience.

To facilitate freedom of movement while maintaining continuity of the application experience, seamless mobility support should enable a mobile user to conduct ongoing tasks, regardless of communication technologies, administrative domains, media types and device models. In addition, security is a fundamental but important requirement for any ready-to-market communication technology, and is also a major concern for end users. However, security measurements inevitably incur computation overhead and processing latency. There is always a tradeoff between performance of seamless handover and security enhancement in handover procedures. In this chapter, we will first analyze the requirements for both seamless roaming and secure communications over heterogenous wireless networks, and then identify and describe the potential challenging issues.

1.1 Requirements for Seamless Roaming

With the explosive popularity of mobile devices, such as the *iPhone*®,[1] *iPad*®,[2] and *Android*™[3] phones, we have witnessed a steady increase in demand for mobile

----

[1] *iPhone* is a trademark of Apple Inc.

[2] *iPad* is a trademark of Apple Inc.

[3] *Android* is a trademark of Google Inc.

J. Cao and C. Zhang, *Seamless and Secure Communications over Heterogeneous Wireless Networks*, SpringerBriefs in Computer Science, DOI 10.1007/978-1-4939-0416-7_1,
© The Author(s) 2014

data services. Research reports released by *Ericsson*[4] in 2011 have found the demand for data service in mobile Internet has actually doubled in the past 12 months [4] and predicted that mobile data traffic will multiply over 10 times by the year 2016, as shown in Fig. 1.1 [6]. The amount of data a consumer uses or requires per day is highly dependent on the user's device. As *Ericsson* reported:

> ..., the mobile data growth patterns reveal that the quality of a smartphone affects which applications people use and the length of time they surf the mobile Internet. [3]

In addition, mobile users also expect to connect to the Internet for communication and access to services through the best suitable connection, anywhere and at anytime. Although the seamless roaming capability is well supported in conventional cellular communication networks, roaming and interworking technologies are still immature in heterogenous wireless networks. Seamless roaming over heterogenous wireless networks will be an ongoing and improved process, due to the requirements from both end users and network administrators.

From the perspective of mobile users, due to the availability of numerous neighboring wireless access networks belonging to different administrative domains, mobile users cannot always identify at every instance which network is the best one to access for theirs services. It is highly demanded to establish a network architecture which can facilitate mobile terminals to access the appropriate networks in a cost-effective way. If a mobile user wants to move from one network to another with continuous services, the terminals have to cope with network changes to maintain services seamlessly. Quality of service is a major issue that the end user should be provided with the service satisfying the user's requirement, while the network workload and cost should not be too much increased. In addition, since end users are provided with numerous services ranging from Voice-over-IP

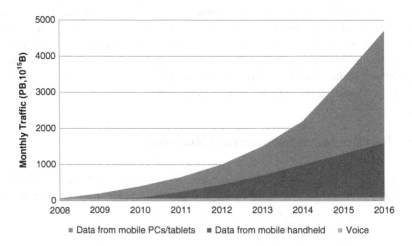

Fig. 1.1 Status and prediction of mobile data demand by Ericsson, reprinted from [3]

---

[4]*Ericsson* is the trademark or registered trademark of Telefonaktiebolaget LM Ericsson.

to Video-on-Demand services, it is expected that users can experience the same quality for all the different services. Therefore, the network architecture need to be designed in such a way that the quality mechanism is incorporated so that users are served according to their individual QoS requirements.

From the perspective of network administrators, due to the availability of multiple wireless access technologies, the network infrastructure need to assist mobile users in identifying the best network at any given instance. This selection of networks have to be done dynamically and to consider a number of theoretical and practical issues, such as the system capacity in terms of the bandwidth upper-bound and the number of simultaneous users that can be supported. Handover management is another concept coming into existence to handle mobility of users roaming between access networks or technologies. When mobile terminals move from one access network to another, mobility mechanisms have to ensure that these sessions are not lost, and that the information after roaming can be forwarded to users, even if they have moved to another access network. Handover management provides guidelines for networks and/or users to follow procedures and mechanisms for seamless transition of services during roaming.

1.2 Requirements for Secure Communications

Securing users' assets is an important objective for security architectures and protection solutions for future heterogeneous wireless networks. Security is a fundamental service of mobile network operators and the security requirements should be fulfilled whenever and wherever mobile services are provided. Due to the exposure of IP-based core networks to tremendous number of mobile terminals, network operators need to provide security solutions to avoid, detect and defend all sorts of possible attacks.

Security of future heterogeneous wireless networks can generally be categorized into two parts, naming terminal security and access network security, providing at mobile terminals and at wireless access networks, respectively. Therefore, it is a joint task for all the participants involved in future mobile environments, including wireless network operators, mobile users themselves, mobile device manufactures and regulatory bodies. In the remaining part of this book, we will focus on the security issues at the network and user sides.

From the perspective of network administrators, infrastructure security should support the functionality of preventing compromise on the network and its components. For any commercial wireless technology, security requirements should first be considered in the initial stage of drafting standards and specifications. For example, in 3GPP Release 99 which is the first release to specify the UMTS 3G networks, there was a specification [1] describing the security threats and requirements in future UMTS networks. In general, the following three operations need to be implemented for security enhancement.

- **Authentication**: for the system to authenticate the origins of both in-coming and out-going data or signaling flows.
- **Integrity**: for the system to detect the unauthorized modification of users' data or signaling traffic.
- **Confidentiality**: for the system to prevent disclosing users' data or signaling, and protect users' privacy.

From the perspective of mobile users, the user experience is a key factor. Security mechanisms should be both intelligent, to handle most requests without the user's intervention, and sufficiently user-friendly with simple configuration steps for end users. In addition, security mechanisms should not be seen to degrade QoS performance, otherwise the execution of continuous services could be disrupted, which may cause user reluctance to adopt security mechanisms.

1.3   Challenges and Issues

As mentioned before, technologies and solutions have been established in conventional wireless cellular networks after the evolution of several generations. The technologies includes seamless mobility in a single administrative domain, high security level and privacy protection, and business-oriented QoS support. Pervasive access and ubiquitous connectivity are offered to mobile subscribers over large-scale areas, and different mobility requirements are also satisfied in different scenarios ranging from high-velocity movement in vehicular networks to stationary access in indoor environments.

However, most wireless communication technologies used in heterogeneous wireless networks are not initially designed with such features. Taking IEEE 802.11 WLAN as an example, its specifications only focus on the Physical (PHY) layer and Medium Access Control (MAC) layer, and WLAN terminals need to obtain IP connectivity to external IP networks, such as the public Internet or a private corporation intranet. Instead of providing large-scale coverage in cellular networks, WLANs are usually sparsely deployed in public or private hotspots, as most of these areas are located in an indoor environment.

Different radio access and data forwarding technologies adopted in heterogeneous wireless networks have imposed several challenges to interoperability and interworking [5]. First, due to different low-layer communication technologies and protocols, access networks in future heterogeneous wireless networks present distinct characteristics in regard to handover management, mobility management, security guarantee and Quality of Service (QoS) provisioning. These issues should be carefully considered while developing interworking strategies to achieve seamless and secure roaming in heterogeneous wireless networks.

Second, with the rapid development of wireless access technologies, mobility management should be made independently to the evolution of wireless communication technologies, and be cooperative with all-IP core networks. Therefore, state-of-the-art technologies in mobility management still have room to be improved in terms of multi-objective handover, ubiquitous wireless access, and QoS guarantee for diverse mobile Internet applications.

We summarize the challenges and issues in the following three subsections.

1.3.1 Mobility Management and Handover Control

A variety of wireless access technologies are available in heterogeneous and ubiquitous network environments. Heterogeneity exists in different levels of networking, such as network architecture, interface protocols, AAA (Authentication, Authorization, Accounting) administration, and QoS provision. Heterogeneity is also reflected in the functional features of different technologies, such as network coverage, data rate and mobility support. Ubiquity is not only presented in a variety of access methods, but also in integration of and cooperation between these heterogeneous wireless technologies. For mobility management, considering ubiquitous support, the main challenges stem from many aspects, including

- Proposing a new generic mobility management architecture, that supports the characteristics of heterogeneity and ubiquity,
- Defining signaling interactions and cooperation between different network entities in the above architecture, including the control plane signaling and data plane signaling,
- Integrating distributed and centralized strategies of mobility management,
- Developing efficient and reliable location update and destination searching algorithms to minimize location management cost according to the hierarchy of distributed location databases and different mobility patterns of mobile users.

The research on roaming technologies over heterogeneous wireless networks mainly focuses on vertical handover techniques among different wireless access technologies. The objective is to maximize handover performance and reliability, while achieving load balance between different cells and networks. The main challenges are

- Designing efficient and feasible handover decision algorithms, taking into consideration of characteristics and multiple requirements from different networks, terminals and applications,
- Designing practical mechanisms for handover execution, which can be initialized by the network side and terminal side, according to the network load and performance or users' preferences and QoS requirements,
- Achieving balance between generality and performance of handover strategies. To be independent to the wireless communication technologies, handover mechanisms are usually designed and implemented in upper layers. This inevitably incurs performance degradation, such as long handover latency. Therefore, a cross-layer design approaches should be introduced into the handover mechanism.

1.3.2   Enhanced Security Management

Due to the open wireless channels and all-IP core networks, security issues in mobility management for heterogeneous wireless networks are much more complex than in traditional closed cellular networks. A reconfigurable, self-adaptive and light-weight security mechanism is needed for future mobility management, which imposes the following challenges.

- Developing integrated and efficient authentication technology.
  In current inter-technology or inter-domain roaming scenarios, there is a high operation and maintenance cost to achieve dual authentication between two access networks. To reduce handover latency and promote service quality, new authentication mechanisms need to increase efficiency in mobile access and handover procedures.
- Establishing trust relationship between mobile users.
  Since a variety of wireless access technologies are adopted in heterogeneous wireless networks, mobile terminals will also be heterogeneous in terms of distribution and management of authentication keys and encryption algorithms. Trust relationship needs to established for cooperation between mobile terminals.
- Developing effective and secure firewall traversal technology.
  To avoid being interrupted by a firewall during inter-domain roaming, mobility management solutions should adopt firewall traversal technology to achieve end-to-end connectivity between communication pairs.

1.3.3   Interoperability and Interworking

Interoperability is the key consideration of mobility management in heterogeneous wireless networks, which incorporate different networking technologies, such as location management, handover strategy, security management, and adopt different mobility mechanisms, such as session mobility and service mobility. The objective of interoperability is to resolve the above differences in heterogeneous wireless networks. More specifically, the following issues need to be addressed.

- Security context mapping in access authentication.
  Since different encryption algorithms and authentication protocols are adopted in heterogeneous wireless networks, it is a challenging problem to map the securities in corresponding networks.
- End-to-end QoS mapping in heterogeneous wireless networks.
  Different architectures and QoS control mechanisms are adopted in heterogeneous wireless networks. It is a challenging problem to map efficiently the QoS requirements and control mechanisms to guarantee the quality of seamless roaming when vertical handover occurs.

- Session context mapping in session mobility.
  Since a different network environment and terminal capability exist in heterogeneous wireless networks, session context mapping will facilitate smoother session mobility and a better user experience.

From the definition by 3GPP[2], interworking refers to the utilization of resources and access to services within the 3GPP system by the WLAN user equipment and user respectively. In 3GPP TR 22.934 [2], a flexible, general and scalable approach was proposed and six interworking scenarios are defined, from a simple interworking scenario between 3GPP networks and WLAN to a fully seamless scenario for inter-system convergence.

Scenario-1: Common Billing and Customer Care.
This is the simplest scheme of 3GPP and WLAN interworking. The connection between the WLAN and 3GPP system is that there is a single customer relationship.
Scenario-2: 3GPP system based Access Control and Charging.
This is the scenario where authentication, authorization and accounting are provided by the 3GPP system. The security level of these functions applied to WLAN is in line with that of the 3GPP system.
Scenario-3: Access to 3GPP system PS based services.
3G packet-switched services are also open to users attached to the WLAN, such as MMS, WAP service, IP multimedia and location-based services.
Scenario-4: Service Continuity.
The goal of this scenario is to allow the services supported in Scenario 3 to survive a change of access between WLAN and 3GPP systems.
Scenario-5: Seamless Services.
The target of this scenario is to provide seamless service continuity between access technologies, for the services supported in Scenario 3.
Scenario-6: Access to 3GPP CS Services.
This scenario allows access to services provided by the entities of the 3GPP Circuit Switched Core Network over WLAN. This scenario does not imply any circuit-switched type of characteristics to be included into WLAN.

The specifications did not set any constraints on the physical topology or logic structure of WLAN, so it can cover most of the roaming scenarios in a interworking between heterogenous wireless networks. However for implementation, there is still much performance improvement to be done.

References

1. 3GPP: Ts 21.133: Universal mobile telecommunications system (umts); security threats and requirements (1999)
2. 3GPP: Tr 22.934 feasibility study on 3gpp system to wireless local area network (wlan) interworking (2011)

3. Ericsson: Mobile data traffic growth doubled over one year (2011). URL http://www.ericsson. com/news/111012_mobile_data_traffic_244188808_c
4. Malik, O.: Mobile data traffic doubled in past 12 months (2011). URL http://gigaom.com/ broadband/mobile-data-traffic-doubled-in-past-12-months/
5. Song, W., Zhuang, W., Saleh, A.: Interworking of 3g cellular networks and wireless lans. Int. J. Wire. Mob. Comput. 2(4), 237–247 (2007). DOI 10.1504/IJWMC.2007.016718. URL http://dx. doi.org/10.1504/IJWMC.2007.016718
6. WILKES, J.: Ericsson: Mobile data traffic will grow 10-fold by 2016 (2011). URL http://www. broadband-expert.co.uk/blog/broadband-news/ericsson-mobile-data-traffic-will-grow-10-fold -by-2016

Chapter 2
Heterogeneous Wireless Networks

In this chapter, we will review the underlying mechanisms for the evolution of wireless communication networks. We will first discuss macro-cellular technologies used in traditional telecommunication systems, and then introduce some micro-cellular technologies as a recent advance in the telecommunications industry. Finally, we will describe existing interworking techniques available in literature and in standardization, including loosely and tightly coupled, I-WLAN and IEEE 802.21.

2.1 Macro-cellular Technologies

The term macro-cell is used to describe cells with larger sizes. A macro-cell is a cell in mobile phone networks that provide radio coverage served by a high power cellular base station. The antennas for macro-cells are mounted on ground-based masts and other existing structures, at a height that provides a clear view over the surrounding buildings and terrain. Macro-cell base stations have power outputs of typically tens of watts [18]. Most wireless communication systems maintained by traditional mobile network operators are powered by macro-cellular technologies.

2.1.1 1G/2G/3G Networks

In the 1980s, the 1G wireless communication system came to the mobile communication environment, which provided a data speed of 2.4 Kbps to support data communication with mobile phones. An example is Nordic Mobile Telephone (NMT). However, this generation still worked in analog system and there were tight limitations in terms of the system capacity and data rate.

J. Cao and C. Zhang, *Seamless and Secure Communications over Heterogeneous Wireless Networks*, SpringerBriefs in Computer Science, DOI 10.1007/978-1-4939-0416-7_2,
© The Author(s) 2014

In the last decades of the last century, 2G wireless communication systems with increased capacity and higher speed gradually replaced the previous generation through technology development and performance enhancement. It was worth noting that 2G wireless systems supported digital communication, such as in Global System for Mobile Communication (GSM). After the transition to the 2G systems, some protocols were developed to increase the data speed that produced the 2.5G wireless systems. The General Packet Radio Service (GPRS), the most common one of those protocols, provided a speed up to 144 Kbps. Later on, the 2.75G wireless system came with a higher data rate than previous generations and provided more enhanced performance in terms of high speed in data service. For example, by adopting advanced coding schemes and transmission mechanisms, Enhanced Data rates for GSM Evolution (EDGE) achieved higher bit-rates per radio channel, resulting in a threefold increase in capacity and performance compared with an ordinary GSM/GPRS connection.

In the late 1990s, the 3G wireless communication system emerged with better multimedia capability and greater networking speed to meet the ever-increasing demand on data services. There are several widely used protocols and standards in the 3G systems, including UMTS, WCDMA, CDMA2000/EVDO, CDMA2000/EVDV, CDMA2000/EVDO-Rev A. In addition, for the economic concern, telecommunication operators usually adopted the evolution by efficiently integrating both 3G and previous generations to reduce the upgrade cost. Beyond 3G system was developed to improve the performance the conventional 3G system and provide a higher speed of up to 14.4 Mbps. As one of the technologies in the 3.5G wireless communication system, High Speed Downlink Packet Access (HSDPA) provides a dramatic performance improvement, based on the bandwidth's substantial increase and support more applications, such as graphics-intensive web browsing, on-demand video playing and multi-user video conferencing.

2.1.2 4G Networks

In the early twenty-first century, some telecommunication operators began to upgrade the 3G to 4G wireless communication systems, which provide a more comprehensive commercialized communication solution with a much higher data rate and better system performance, in terms of high reception ratio, low packet loss ratio and low packet delivery latency. International Telecommunication Union (ITU) has stated that 4G technologies require a data transmission rate of at least 100 Mbps while a user moves at high speed and a much high data rate up to 1 Gbps in a fixed location to support better multimedia applications, such as video-on-demand services. There are several challenges to achieve such performance criteria in mobile scenarios, including routing optimization technique, fast handover technique, integration technique between Mobile IP and cellular IP, multi-path technique, mobility management technique for all-IP networks.

In October 2010, ITU Radiocommunication Sector (ITU-R) completed the assessment of six candidate proposals for the future 4G mobile wireless broadband technology, called IMT-Advanced. Among these candidates, two technologies were accorded as the official designation of IMT-Advanced, including WirelessMAN-Advanced and LTE-Advanced.

WiMAX (Worldwide Interoperability for Microwave Access) is a telecommunication protocol [12], which is designed to deliver next-generation, high-speed mobile voice and data services and wireless *last-mile* backhaul connections that could potentially displace a great deal of existing radio air network infrastructure. The first version of IEEE 802.16 Standard was released in 2001, and defined the basic air interface specification for wireless metropolitan area networks (MANs). Subsequently, physical layer technologies, such as orthogonal frequency division multiplexing (OFDM) and orthogonal frequency division multiple access (OFDMA), and new features, such as power-saving, idle mode, handover and an improved OFDMA physical layer, were amended to the original draft. The WirelessMAN-Advanced specification was incorporated in IEEE 802.16 standard beginning with approval of IEEE 802.16m standard.

In the evolution tree of mobile communication technologies, LTE (Long Term Evolution) is considered to be the latest standard, whose first release was published in March 2009 and is referred to as LTE Release 8 [2]. 3GPP has developed the LTE standard for 4G wireless communication systems based on orthogonal frequency-division multiplexing (OFDM) waveform for downlink and single-carrier FDM (SC-FDM) waveform for uplink communications, mainly to improve the user experience for broadband data communications [6]. The LTE-Advanced specification was developed by 3GPP as LTE Release 10 and Beyond.

To conclude this section, we summarize the generations of cellular networks with mainstream technologies in Table 2.1.

2.2 Micro-cellular Technologies

Compared to macro-cellular wireless networks, micro-cellular networks are served by low power base stations or access points to cover smaller areas, such as an office, and support a fewer number of mobile users. Typically, the range covered by micro-cell networks is less than 2 km wide. The flexibility of cell size is a significant factor contributing to capacity improvement, and power controlling can largely reduce the interference from neighboring cells in the overlapping radio frequencies.

2.2.1 IEEE 802.11 Based WLAN

IEEE 802.11 based WLAN is the most popular micro-cellular wireless communication system in the world. However, WLAN technology was not initially

Table 2.1 Generations of cellular networks

Generations	Protocols	Data rate	Features
1G	AMPS NMT TACS	N/A	• Only support voice service • No data service
2G	CDMA GSM PHS	Up to 20 Kbps	• Digital voice service • Push-to-talk (PTT) • Short message service (SMS) • Conference calling • Simple data applications such as email and web browsing
2.5G	GPRS CDMA2000 1×RTT	114 Kbps (30–40 Kbps) 144 Kbps (60–80 Kbps)	All 2G features plus: • MMS (multimedia message service) • Web browsing • Real-time location-based services, such as directions • Basic multimedia, including support for short audio and video clips, games and images
2.75G	 EDGE EGPRS IMT-SC	384 Kbps 473 Kbps (uplink)/1.2 Mbps (downlink) 600 Kbps	• Better performance for all 2/2.5G service
3G	WCDMA CDMA2000 /EVDO CDMA2000 /EVDO-RevA TD-SCDMA	2 Mbps 2.4 Mbps 3.1 Mbps 2.8 Mbps	Support for all prior 2G and 2.5G features plus: • Full motion video • Streaming music • 3D gaming • Fast web browsing
3.5G	HSDPA/HSUPA CDMA2000 /EVDO-RevB	14.4 Mbps 46 Mbps	Support for all prior 2/2.5/3G features plus: • On-demand video • Video conferencing • Faster web browsing (especially graphics intensive sites)
4G	WiMAX UMB LTE	100 Mbps 35 Mbps 100 Mps	Support for all prior 2G/3G features plus: • High quality streaming video • High quality Video conferencing • High quality Voice-over-IP (VoIP)

designed for short range communication. When the proprietary Direct Sequence Spread Spectrum (DSSS) technology over 900 MHz was adopted, it could set up quite a long distant link providing data throughput of 860 Kbps. In 1990s, the working frequency of WLAN was set to 2.4 GHz and it could support a higher data throughput of 1 Mbps or 2 Mbps in a shorter distance. The year 1992 witnessed the start of drafting of the IEEE 802.11 standard for wireless LAN technologies, which had proposed 1 Mbps as a standard data rate and 2 Mbps as a Turbo mode. Since then, a series of IEEE 802.11 standards have been proposed to improve the performance of WLAN, some of which are listed as follows.

- IEEE 802.11a: IEEE 802.11a-1999 High-speed Physical Layer in the 5 GHz band
- IEEE 802.11b: IEEE 802.11b-1999 Higher Speed Physical Layer Extension in the 2.4 GHz band
- IEEE 802.11d: an approved amendment to the IEEE 802.11 specification that adds support for additional regulatory domains
- IEEE 802.11e: an approved amendment to the IEEE 802.11 standard that defines QoS Enhancements, including packet bursting
- IEEE 802.11g: IEEE 802.11g-2003: Further Higher Data Rate Extension in the 2.4 GHz Band
- IEEE 802.11h: an approved amendment to IEEE 802.11 standard that adds Spectrum and Transmit Power Management Extensions
- IEEE 802.11i: an approved amendment to the original IEEE 802.11 that specifies security mechanisms for wireless networks and implements WPA2
- IEEE 802.11n: an approved amendment to the IEEE 802.11 standard to improve network throughput using multiple input multiple output (MIMO) technology
- IEEE 802.11p: an approved amendment to the IEEE 802.11 standard to support Wireless Access for the Vehicular Environment
- IEEE 802.11r: an approved amendment to the IEEE 802.11 standard to permit continuous connectivity aboard wireless devices in motion, with fast and secure handovers from one access point to another, managed in a seamless manner
- IEEE 802.11s: an approved amendment to the IEEE 802.11 standard to support mesh networking
- IEEE 802.11u: an approved amendment to the IEEE 802.11 standard to add features that improve interworking with external networks.

The 802.11 standards define two types of communication modes: infrastructure mode and ad hoc mode. In infrastructure mode, the wireless network consists of a wireless access point (AP) and multiple wireless clients. The AP acts as a base station and is also responsible for security management. All wireless clients communicate with external networks through the access point, which provides the connection from the wireless communication media to the hard-wired communication media. Since the wireless communication media is open, all wireless clients within the communication range can receive the packets. But in the default protocol operation, only those clients with the appropriate destination address will handle the packets.

In the ad hoc mode, the wireless network is only comprised of IEEE 802.11 wireless clients, which communicate directly with each other without forwarding packets to a access point. This mode is convenient for quickly setting up a wireless network in a meeting room, hotel conference center, or anywhere else where sufficient wired infrastructure does not exist.

2.2.2 Wireless Mesh Network

A wireless mesh network (WMN) is a new wireless communications network consisting of mesh routers, mesh clients and gateways, which are self-organized in mesh topology. Wireless mesh networks can be implemented with various wireless technology, including IEEE 802.11, IEEE 802.15, IEEE 802.16, cellular technologies, or combinations of more than one type. Wireless mesh networking is a promising technology for next-generation wireless communication systems, with the capability of rapid deployment and flexible reconfigurability for disaster recovery, convention centers and hard-to-wire areas. WMN is also an alternative for long-term network infrastructure to extend wireless broadband access in dense urban areas and low-cost backbone networking to Internet gateway in remote rural areas (Fig. 2.1).

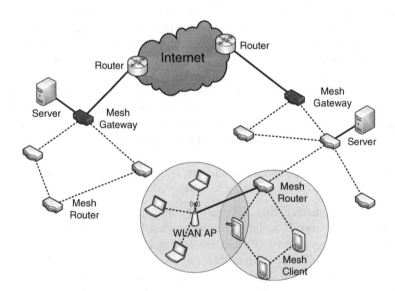

Fig. 2.1 Wireless mesh networks

There are three kinds of network structures in wireless mesh networks, including infrastructure-based WMN, client-based WMN and hybrid WMN. In the first architecture, mesh routers establish a backbone network with the wireless technologies, and mesh clients obtain the network access through the core network.

If some of the mesh routers have a connection to the Internet via wireless or wired links, they can be set to be the gateways, which provide the entire network Internet access service. In addition, mesh routers are usually stationary in the whole network. In client-based WMNs, it allows peer-to-peer networking between mesh clients, with no dedicated mesh routers. To a certain extent from network topology aspect, a client-based WMN is the same as a traditional ad hoc network. To meet diverse requirements of different application scenarios, a hybrid WMN is proposed to combine the above two networks.

The characteristics of WMNs [3] are listed as follows:

- **Multi-hop and ad hoc wireless networking**.
  One of the most important features in wireless mesh networks is its multi-hop and ad hoc wireless networking technology to forward data packets, which can effectively extend the network coverage constrained by a single base station in WLAN, and achieve non-line-of-sight propagation, which is impossible for high radio frequency.

- **Capability of self-organization and self-healing**.
  Due to the distributed nature of multi-hop and ad hoc networking, WMN can simplify network design and deployment, thus reduce network construction and maintenance costs. WMNs can also upgrade network performance in terms of load balance and fault tolerance. Due to these features, WMNs have low initial construction costs, and can be deployed in an incremental fashion.

- **Various mobility and access patterns of mesh nodes**.
  Different mobility patterns exist in WMNs, including the stationary mesh routers and moving mesh clients. In addition, there are also different network access patterns, including only peer-to-peer communication between mesh routers, and hybrid communications among mesh clients. All these differences will require different protocol design and strategy adoption.

- **Different Power-consumption constraints for mesh nodes**.
  Mesh routers are almost stationary, and usually do not have much constraints on power consumption. However, mobile mesh clients are powered by battery and may meet the power efficiency requirements. Thus, the MAC or routing protocols optimized for mesh routers need to not be appropriate for mesh clients.

- **Compatibility and interoperability with existing wireless networks**.
  Since WMN can be implemented in multiple wireless communication technologies, compatibility and interoperability will be solved in the radio access layer. The researchers may focus on the MAC layer and upper layers to design suitable protocols and applications.

2.2.3 Femtocell

Femtocells are small base stations with low transmission power, and almost all of the cellular functionalities, but a limited coverage to end users in indoor environments, such as houses and offices. Femtocells connect to core networks of service providers via broadband Internet connections. A femtocell allows service coverage extended to indoor environments, especially where wireless access would be limited or unavailable, without expensive deployment cost. Femtocells use the same physical layer technology as cellular networks and are standardized since 3GPP release 8, where it is called Home NodeB (HNB) in WCDMA systems and Home eNodeB (H(e)NB) in LTE systems (Fig. 2.2).

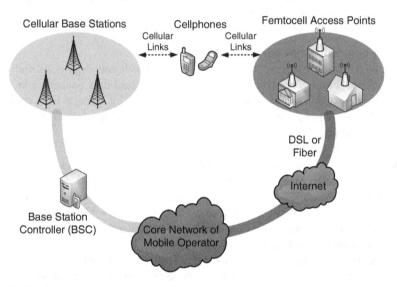

Fig. 2.2 Femtocell networks

The key benefits of femtocells [5] are summarized as follows.

- **Larger coverage and higher capacity.**
  Due to their low power transmission, femtocells can largely avoid interference between other co-channel signals, and provide a high quality communication channel for mobile users. Therefore, femtocells improve spectral efficiency in terms of user numbers per unit coverage. In addition, due to the short distance to base station, mobile terminals can also achieve energy efficiency by lowering transmission power and prolonging battery life.
- **Improved macro-cell reliability.**
  In the presence of femtocells serving indoor mobile clients, macro-cellular networks can provide much more reliable data service for outdoor mobile users, due to the reduced overhead required to handle poor signals from indoor users.
- **Reduced deployment and maintenance cost.**
  Femtocell can be deployed with reduced construction and maintenance costs for networks operators. As reported by a research study dated in 2007, the maintenance cost drops from $60,000 per year per macro-cell base station to just $200 per year per femtocell base station [4].

- **Decreased subscriber turnover**.
  Poor in-building coverage causes customer dissatisfaction, encouraging customers to either switch operators, or maintain a separate wired line whenever indoors. The enhanced home coverage provided by femtocells will decrease the motivation for home users to switch carriers.

2.3   Interworking Technologies

Interworking architectures between heterogeneous wireless networks can be divided into two main categories: loose and tightly coupled architectures. For the convenience of description, we will take interworking between 3G networks and WLANs as examples. We first briefly introduce the above two architectures, and then present two standard implementations for interworking between these two types of wireless networks, including I-WLAN interworking solution from 3GPP, and Media Independent Handover from IEEE.

2.3.1   Loosely Coupled Architecture

In a loosely coupled architecture, interconnected wireless networks are relatively independent from each other in terms of handling data flows and signaling messages. There is a common component in all loosely coupled solutions, which is the adoption of Mobile IP as mobility management protocol to integrate multiple wireless networking systems. A typical loosely coupled architecture is shown in Fig. 2.3.

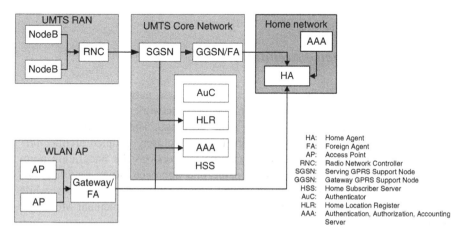

Fig. 2.3 System architecture of loosely coupled approach

Since the concerned networks are usually independent of each other, the internal operations in each network can easily migrate to the interworking scenarios nearly without modification. Therefore, the improvement on roaming performance is almost developed in the interaction part between two networks. Some approaches [10] are listed below.

1. **Effective handover initiation and accurate handover decision**
   This approach aims at determining when mobile clients take handover, and which access network mobile clients connect to after handover. Related work on handover initiation and decision algorithms usually considers various parameters from both the client and network sides, including the received signal strength of the current access network at the client side, the current dominant traffic pattern, and handover overhead from different networks.

2. **Optimization on Mobile IP procedures**
   In standardized Mobile IP protocols, there exists several signal interactions between three participants in the whole procedure. The main objective of the optimization on Mobile IP procedures is to shorten the delay caused by the execution of the protocols related to Mobile IP operations. Some proposed mechanisms have been proposed to reduce the handover latency by improving the efficiency of signaling passing in both intra-domain and inter-domain scenarios, or by utilizing cross-layer information to capture the accurate handover trigger.

3. **Policy-based solutions**
   Different from the approach 1 using real network metrics to predict handover occurrences, policy-based solutions evaluate handover behaviors by the information derived from policy-based criteria, including the jitter requirement for on-line video streaming applications, the security capabilities of terminal for high-confidential applications. To obtain the complex network context from different wireless access networks, they propose new network entities between different network operators, such as context management, handover decisions, and interoperability.

2.3.2 Tightly Coupled Architecture

In a tightly coupled architecture, non-cellular wireless networks, such as IEEE 802.11 based WLANs, are connected to the core network of cellular networks as access networks to provide cellular radio coverage. There are two common approaches to achieve mobility management in the closely coupled architecture, namely reuse of some functionality in cellular networks as the integration point and adoption of Mobile IP protocols. In the first approach, some modifications need to be made to facilitate the additional wireless access technologies, while the other approach needs to deploy new network entities to implement Mobile IP functionality.

According to different degrees of integration between cellular and non-cellular wireless access networks, solutions for the tightly coupled architecture can be categorized into the following three groups, namely coupling at GGSN level, coupling at SGSN level and coupling at RNC level. Among them, coupling at RNC level requires the tightest relationship between the two networks.

2.3.2.1 Coupling at the GGSN Level

One of the tightly coupled solutions to support seamless roaming between UMTS and WLAN is presented in [15], which implements coupling at the GGSN level. In this architecture, as illustrated in Fig. 2.4, a new logical node, called the Virtual GPRS Support Node (VGSN), is designed to interconnect the UMTS and WLAN core networks. VGSN in UMTS networks acts as normal GPRS Support Node (GSN) and is also an access router in WLAN. The main tasks of VGSN are signaling conversion of subscriber/mobility information and data forwarding between the two heterogenous networks.

In this architecture, both networks are independent of each other and handle their own subscribers in coverage separately; VGSN servers as the point of integration to connect two networks. When mobile users roam between UMTS and WLAN networks, VGSN will take charge of the SGSN functionality in the network where the users will move to. In the normal operation mode, the subscriber in WLAN will not generate data traffic to UMTS networks, and data flows caused by UMTS users in UMTS networks will bypass the WLAN. In roaming scenarios, VGSN takes charge of GGSN in UMTS networks, which is between the WLAN gateway and SGSN in the forwarding path of out-going packets to mobile terminals.

The main advantage of the GGSN-level coupling approach is simplicity, in terms of the interactions between two networks and the introduction of additional functionality. For example, the two networks can handle their own subscribers independently until the handover occurs. Mobile IP is not needed, so the system design can be simplified. Moreover, the simulation results in [15] showed that the performance is much better than other tightly coupled solutions. For example, the VGSN approach obtains similar average per-user bandwidth, but significantly lower handover latency compared with amount of Mobile IP based solutions. The main disadvantage of this architecture is that the successful integration of two heterogeneous wireless networks requires a strong roaming agreement between UMTS and WLAN operators, since the VGSN entity does not belong to any network and should be controlled by the administrative party for the cooperation.

2.3.2.2 Coupling at the SGSN Level

In [14] and [13], another type of coupling architecture was proposed at the SGSN level. The key functional entity in the system is the GPRS Interworking Function (GIF), which is connected to a WLAN and to a serving SGSN. The main function of the GIF is to convert the WLAN functionalities to a unified interface to the core network of cellular networks, and to mask the technology heterogeneity of WLAN technology. From the perspective of cellular networks, WLAN is a special radio access network which consists of only one cell. To achieve this goal, the WLAN adaption function (WAF) is developed to identify the time when the WLAN radio subsystem is enabled and to inform the upper layers, which subsequently redirects signaling and data traffic to the WLAN. The WAF is deployed in both mobile stations and on top of GIF functionality. WAF functionality includes hardware management service, location management service, QoS support services. The system architecture of this approach is shown in Fig. 2.5.

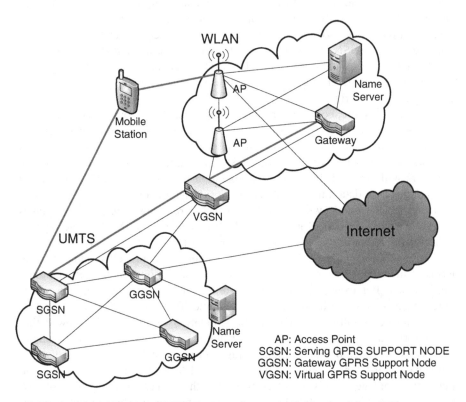

Fig. 2.4 System architecture of GGSN-level coupling approach (Reprinted from [15])

The main advantage of this solution is the enhanced mobility support for roaming across two domains, entirely based on cellular mobility management protocols, which guarantee service continuity including authentication, authorization, accounting, billing systems and other data sources. By reusing the GPRS core network resources, the network deployment cost can also be reduced in terms of

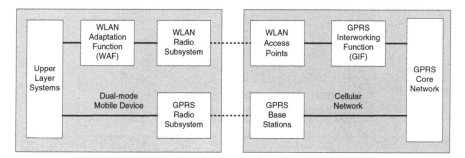

Fig. 2.5 System architecture of SGSN-level coupling approach (Reprinted from [13])

infrastructure with similar functionalities. However, the business model for this kind of coupling is only beneficial to cellular operators, since WLAN only acts as the access part in this architecture. In addition, due to the large amount of WLAN traffic redirected to cellular networks via the SGSN, the core network should be improved to support the new characteristic.

2.3.2.3 Coupling at the RNC Level

The third type of coupling architecture, as proposed in [16], implements the integration of UMTS and WLAN networks at the RNC level. A new network entity, called Inter-Working Unit (IWU), is introduced between the RNC and WLAN, as shown in Fig. 2.6. The IWU functionality is on the network integration and radio access. Some of these modifications imply corresponding modifications of the protocol stack on the mobile terminal. When integration is done on the wireless access networks, there exist several options to forward the signal messages and data flows in both networks. For example, user data in the WLAN can be provided only in the downlink, it can be transferred bidirectionally. The WLAN-related signaling can be exchanged via the WLAN network interface or via the WCDMA interface. An additional distinction includes the fact that access to the network can be provided via the WLAN and WCDMA interfaces simultaneously, or on only one of the interfaces at a time.

The main advantage of this type of architecture is the significant reduction in handover latency, due to the tighter coupling design and functionality reuse in most entities of cellular networks. However, the main drawback is that the architecture is only suitable for network operators deploying both access networks due to the tighter correlation between the two networks. In addition, it requires functionality and protocol modification of both communication systems, which is more complex in system design and implementation.

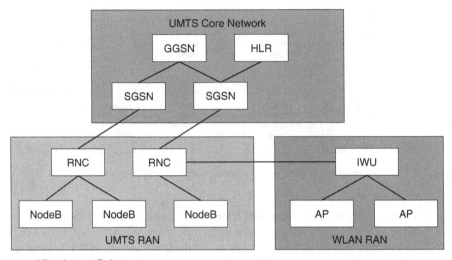

Fig. 2.6 System architecture of RNC-level coupling approach (Reprinted from [16])

2.3.3 Interworking Wireless Local Area Network

The interworking wireless local area network (I-WLAN) was proposed in the 3GPP
Release 6 specifications [1], which provides an integration architecture between
3GPP networks and WLANs. As shown in Fig. 2.7, there are three main entities,
namely a WAG (Wireless Access Gateway), a PDG (Packet Data Gateway) and
a AAA Server. The mobile terminal is typically equipped with multiple network
interfaces, such as 3G radio and Wi-Fi card.

In the coverage of WLANs, the mobile terminal can connect to a WLAN access
network using a Wi-Fi interface card; and out of the coverage, it can switch to 3G
networks, whose service is assumed everywhere. The WAG is a gateway through
which the data to/from the WLAN Access Network shall be routed to provide a
WLAN-interface enabled terminal with 3G packet-switched based services in a
WLAN 3GPP IP Access enabled system. The PDG in the I-WLAN architecture
works as a gateway to 3GPP PS based services, which may be accessed via a Packet
Data Gateway in the user's home network, or via a PDG in the selected visiting
network. When entering into the coverage of a WLAN access network, the mobile
terminal informs the I-WLAN infrastructure of its association thus establishing a
secure tunnel between the mobile terminal and PDG. Packet Switched (PS) domain
signaling and user plane data are carried into this secure tunnel over the air interface.

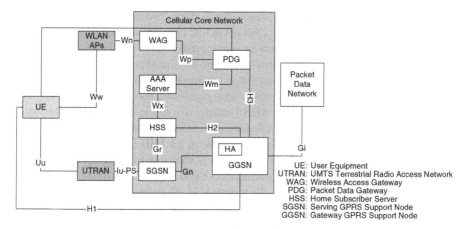

Fig. 2.7 System architecture of I-WLAN interworking (Reprinted from [1])

A new framework for an evolution or migration of the 3GPP system to a higher-data-rate, lower-latency, packet-optimized system, called System Architecture Evolution (SAE), was developed in 3GPP Release 7. To enhance the capability of the 3GPP system to cope with rapid growth in IP data traffic, the packet-switched technology utilized within 3G mobile networks requires further enhancement. Additionally, it is expected that IP-based 3GPP services will be provided through various access technologies. Therefore, I-WLAN is included in the SAE to ensure a smooth migration path from the R6 I-WLAN work to a generic multi-access solution. Apart from seamless mobility across heterogeneous radio access technologies, I-WLAN R7 also supports access to IP Multimedia Subsystem (IMS) and private networks from I-WLAN, LoCation Service (LCS) for I-WLAN in order to enlarge the scope of location-services deployed for GSM/UMTS.

2.3.4 IEEE 802.21 Media Independent Handover

The IEEE Working Group on IEEE 802.21 Standard [8], Media Independent Handover (MIH), is developing a standard to enable handover and interoperability between heterogeneous network types, including both IEEE 802 and non IEEE 802 networks. The standard is proposed for vertical handovers between different network technologies and administrative domains, which can also be used in homogeneous handovers.

The MIH standard comprises a handover-featured framework, a set of handover-enabling functions (MIH Functions – MIHF), and a MIH Service Access Point (MIH SAP and MIH LINK SAP). In MIHF, the functions can be classified into three categories, including the Media-Independent Event Service (MIES), the Media-Independent Command Service (MICS), and the Media-Independent Information

Service (MIIS). MIES provides event classification, event filtering and event reporting corresponding to dynamic changes in link characteristics, links status, and link quality. MICS enables MIH users to manage and control link behavior relevant to handovers and mobility. MIIS provides a two-way channel for all the layers to share necessary information that is useful in making handover decisions[9].

In the MIH framework, information and command services of the mobility management system between other MIHF entities are supported by MIHF through the MIH SAP, which is also responsible for information exchange between the lower layers of access networks surrounding MNs through the MIH LINK SAP primitives. The system architecture of the MIH framework is shown in Fig. 2.8.

It should be mentioned that improvements in the IEEE 802.21 MIH have recently been discussed outside the IEEE working group [7]. More and more extensions and enhancements are first proposed in academic research. For example, an Enhanced Media Independent Handover (EMIH) framework [17] for the original IEEE 802.21 MIH standard was proposed to leverage additional information from higher layers, such as application layers, user context and network context. To achieve this, EMIH considered two important problems from future communication systems, including how to utilize partial information due to incomplete measurements, and how to handle the robustness problem due to inaccurate measurements. Novel algorithms were developed to optimize the decision-making factorsand facilitate handover in

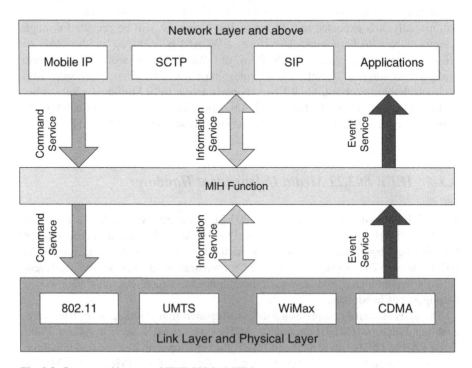

Fig. 2.8 System architecture of IEEE 802.21 MIH framework

heterogeneous wireless networks. Although there were some drawbacks in their system, such as only considering static values in context, the cross-layer design concept of the enhancement framework is an important improvement on the original IEEE 802.11 MIH framework.

In addition, the IEEE 802.21 MIH framework has become the basis to handle the handover between heterogeneous wireless networks, and is considered to be the channel to provide parameter inputs for handover decision-making procedures. For example, a Vertical Handover Decision (VHD) system [11] was proposed to facilitate optimization of overall performance of the integrated system of access networks, specifically in terms of overall battery lifetime and load balancing. In the system, the proposed VHD algorithm is implemented in multiple VHD controllers (VHDCs), which are located in the access networks. From the perspective of the protocol stack on VHDCs, the VHDC algorithm is based on the MIHF layer, which is located above the physical layer and link layer.

References

1. 3GPP: Ts 23.234 v6.10.0 3gpp system to wireless local area network (wlan) interworking; system description (release 6) (2006)
2. 3GPP: Evolved universal terrestrial radio access (e-utra) and evolved universal terrestrial radio access network (e-utran);overall description; stage 2 (release 10) (2009)
3. Akyildiz, I.F., Wang, X., Wang, W.: Wireless mesh networks: a survey. Comput. Netw. ISDN Syst. **47**(4), 445–487 (2005). DOI 10.1016/j.comnet.2004.12.001. URL http://dx.doi.org/10.1016/j.comnet.2004.12.001
4. Analysys: Picocells and femtocells: Will indoor base-stations transform the telecoms industry (2007). URL http://tinyurl.com/a4galjt
5. Chandrasekhar, V., Andrews, J., Gatherer, A.: Femtocell networks: a survey. Communications Magazine, IEEE **46**(9), 59–67 (2008). DOI 10.1109/MCOM.2008.4623708
6. Damnjanovic, A., Montojo, J., Wei, Y., Ji, T., Luo, T., Vajapeyam, M., Yoo, T., Song, O., Malladi, D.: A survey on 3gpp heterogeneous networks. Wireless Communications, IEEE **18**(3), 10–21 (2011). DOI 10.1109/MWC.2011.5876496
7. Fernandes, S., Karmouch, A.: Vertical mobility management architectures in wireless networks: A comprehensive survey and future directions. Communications Surveys Tutorials, IEEE **14**(1), 45–63 (2012). DOI 10.1109/SURV.2011.082010.00099
8. IEEE: IEEE 802.21-2008 – IEEE standard for local and metropolitan area networks – media independent handover services (2008). URL http://standards.ieee.org/findstds/standard/802.21-2008.html
9. IEEE: IEEE standard for local and metropolitan area networks – media independent handover services (2012). URL http://ieeexplore.ieee.org/xpl/articleDetails.jsp?arnumber=STDPD95845&contentType=Standards
10. Lampropoulos, G., Passas, N., Merakos, L., Kaloxylos, A.: Handover management architectures in integrated wlan/cellular networks. Communications Surveys Tutorials, IEEE **7**(4), 30–44 (2005). DOI 10.1109/COMST.2005.1593278
11. Lee, S., Sriram, K., Kim, K., Kim, Y.H., Golmie, N.: Vertical handoff decision algorithms for providing optimized performance in heterogeneous wireless networks. Vehicular Technology, IEEE Transactions on **58**(2), 865–881 (2009). DOI 10.1109/TVT.2008.925301

12. Pareit, D., Lannoo, B., Moerman, I., Demeester, P.: The history of wimax: A complete survey of the evolution in certification and standardization for ieee 802.16 and wimax. Communications Surveys Tutorials, IEEE **14**(4), 1183–1211 (2012). DOI 10.1109/SURV.2011.091511.00129
13. Salkintzis, A.: Interworking techniques and architectures for wlan/3g integration toward 4g mobile data networks. Wireless Communications, IEEE **11**(3), 50–61 (2004). DOI 10.1109/MWC.2004.1308950
14. Salkintzis, A., Fors, C., Pazhyannur, R.: Wlan-gprs integration for next-generation mobile data networks. Wireless Communications, IEEE **9**(5), 112–124 (2002). DOI 10.1109/MWC.2002.1043861
15. Tsao, S.L., Lin, C.C.: Vgsn: a gateway approach to interconnect umts/wlan networks. In: Personal, Indoor and Mobile Radio Communications, 2002. The 13th IEEE International Symposium on, vol. 1, pp. 275–279 vol.1 (2002). DOI 10.1109/PIMRC.2002.1046704
16. Vulic, N., Niemegeers, I., de Groot, S.: Architectural options for the wlan integration at the umts radio access level. In: Vehicular Technology Conference, 2004. VTC 2004-Spring. 2004 IEEE 59th, vol. 5, pp. 3009–3013 Vol.5 (2004). DOI 10.1109/VETECS.2004.1391476
17. Wang, Y., Zhang, P., Zhou, Y., Yuan, J., Liu, F., Li, G.: Handover management in enhanced mih framework for heterogeneous wireless networks environment. Wirel. Pers. Commun. **52**(3), 615–636 (2010). DOI 10.1007/s11277-008-9628-5. URL http://dx.doi.org/10.1007/s11277-008-9628-5
18. Wikipedia: Macrocell (2012). URL http://en.wikipedia.org/wiki/Macrocell

Chapter 3
Seamless Roaming over Heterogeneous Wireless Networks

In this chapter, we describe the technologies for seamless roaming over heterogeneous wireless networks. In the first two sections, we will briefly introduce basic concepts and existing solutions in handover management and mobility management. In the last section, we will present case studies on the roaming technology adopted in our **HAWK** platform, including the context-aware MIH framework and UDP-tunnel based Mobile IP.

3.1 Handover Management

As a fundamental service in any mobile network, handover management is defined as a kind of network capability supporting continuous communications for mobile users, no matter where users are, which access networks are associated with and what kind of wireless technologies are adopted. The main objective is to preserve the communication channel with specified quality during the users' handover.

According to different entities involved in the handover decision-making procedure, three main approaches of handover management are commonly adopted in standards and industries, namely network-controlled handover, mobile-assisted handover, and mobile-controlled handover. In the first approach, network-side entities make handover decisions based on the signal measurements of mobile terminals, which are collected by the network at a number of access points or base stations. In the second approach, mobile terminals perform measurements at the client side and report the results to the network, which then makes the handover decision. In the above two approaches, since the network is the final decision maker for users' handover, network-side entities can adopt additional mechanisms to improve the network performance, such as reallocating the number of users in different serving areas.

J. Cao and C. Zhang, *Seamless and Secure Communications over Heterogeneous Wireless Networks*, SpringerBriefs in Computer Science, DOI 10.1007/978-1-4939-0416-7_3, © The Author(s) 2014

In mobile-controlled handover, mobile terminals can make the final decision to select the candidate networks according to their own measurements. Since it is fully distributed from the aspect of decision-making entities, this approach may affect network performance in terms of fairness, stability, and security. In recent research, a new approach, called network-assisted handover, is emerging. A mobile terminal does not only collect the results from its own measurements, but also obtain information from the network. Compared to fully mobile-controlled handover, handover performance will be improved in terms of communication continuity and system capacity.

The entire handover process can be divided into three main phases, namely handover initiation, handover decision and handover execution. Handover initiation is responsible for searching available access networks and triggering handover. During the handover decision, decision algorithms are executed to find the most appropriate candidate networks according to different communication metrics. Finally, the handover execution is carried out to exchange signaling messages for communication re-connection and data forwarding through the new connection. In the following sub-sections, we will introduce the three phases in more details.

3.1.1   Handover Initialization

In the handover initialization phase, network discovery plays an import role in preparing the handover. In wireless communication standards, the network discovery functionality has been implemented by several approaches, including out-of-band mechanisms, link layer advertisements and network layer information. In RFC 3017, the Roaming Access eXtensible Markup Language (XML) Document Type Definition (DTD) was proposed to describe the attributes of points of presence and Internet service providers. The XML DTD also included hints as to the appropriate network access identifier to be used with a particular point of presence. However, this out-of-band pre-configuration has become increasingly inefficient when access networks and points of attachment have proliferated. It is very difficult to maintain the latest list of points of attachment in a complex network.

In IEEE 802.11 based WLAN, the Beacon and Probe Request/Response mechanism provides a way for wireless clients to discover access points and their capabilities. According to the IEEE 802.11 standards, a unique network identifier of WLAN, namely Service Set Identifier (SSID), is included in both Beacon and Probe Response frames. There exist two network discovery modes for wireless clients, passive scan mode and active scan mode. In the passive scan mode, wireless clients periodically listen for Beacon frames and handle those frames to check the available access networks, while in the active scan mode, they send out Probe Request frames and wait for Probe Response frames from nearby networks.

During the process of network discovery, attributes and capabilities of access networks can be also typically discovered, as shown in Fig. 3.1 and are listed below.

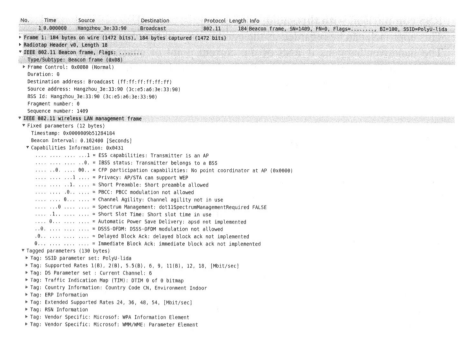

Fig. 3.1 IEEE 802.11 Beacon frame structure captured by *Wireshark*

- Access network name (e.g., IEEE 802.11 SSID)
- Supported data rates (e.g., 1 Mbps for IEEE 802.11b, 18 Mbps for IEEE802.11g)
- Wireless security mechanisms (e.g., Wired Equivalent Privacy (WEP), Wi-Fi Protected Access (WPA), WPA2)
- Quality of Service capabilities (e.g., IEEE 802.11e support)

To trigger a handover process, the received signal strength (RSS) has widely been used as an indicator of the condition to start a handover procedure. Some of the commonly used approaches are summarized as follows.

- **RSS only**
  In this approach, the RSS is the only metric use to initialize the handover process. A handover happens if RSS of the current point of attachment is less than a predefined threshold T ($RSS_{current} < T$). For example, the default triggering mechanism in IEEE 802.11 standard follows this approach.
- **RSS comparison**
  In this approach, the RSS values of the current point of attachment and other candidates are compared to determine whether a handover process should be initiated. The handover occurs if RSS of the candidate point of attachment is greater than the current one ($RSS_{current} < RSS_{candidate}$). Sometimes, there is an additional pre-defined threshold H in order to alleviate the ping-pong effect ($RSS_{current} + H < RSS_{candidate}$).

- **RSS comparison with threshold**

  This approach can be regarded as the combination of the above two approaches. The handover happens if RSS of the current point of attachment is less than a predefined threshold T, and the RSS of the candidate point of attachment is greater than the current one ($RSS_{current} < T$ and $RSS_{current} + H < RSS_{candidate}$).

3.1.2 Handover Decision

In heterogeneous wireless networks, it is a common case that several overlapping wireless access networks coexist with different wireless communication technologies. When a mobile device moves in such wireless environment, the first challenge it may face is how to select the most appropriate target network from a number of different wireless access networks. These networks may belong to the same or different administrative domains, which support a diverse set of networking capabilities, in terms of coverage, bandwidth, latency, pricing, etc. The handover decision dominates the network selection process and determines the best target network based on the decision criteria provided by the device, the application and the monitoring process. In a simplest way, a single parameter, such as RSS, is mainly adopted to make the handover decision by network administrator to achieve mobility management.

In order to enhance the basic handover decision mechanism, various algorithms and protocols have been proposed to find the optimal selection in the research literature. In general, the network selection problem can be formulated as a complex decision-making problem and may involve multiple static or dynamic parameters, criteria, objectives in the decision process.

There are two major categories in handover decision, namely centralized and decentralized approaches. In the centralized approach, a centralized, operator-controlled decision algorithm is deployed at the network side and operators are able to make the final decision to establish the association between access networks and mobile terminals. Most of the telecommunication operators adopt this solution in their cellular networks. For the other approach, mobile users control the decision-making process and can select the best network manually or automatically following the predefined policies. For example, the Wi-Fi network is a typical scenario adopting decentralized approach. Wi-Fi users can freely choose the target network according to their profiles. In the following two subsections, we will discuss two important components for the handover decision, called decision criteria and decision-making algorithms.

3.1.2.1 Decision Criteria

The decision criteria are used to feed the input of decision-making algorithms to choose the best target network for mobile clients. There are four major categories of those decision criteria in network selection process, including

- **Network Attributes**, including information related to the technical and administrative attributes of the access networks, such as the type of the wireless technology, security levels, network average/peak load, available bandwidth, delivery latency, signal quality, roaming capability, pricing scheme.
- **Terminal Information**, including hardware and software information about mobile users' devices, such as computation capability, screen size and resolution, available network interfaces, location information, remaining battery power.
- **Application Requirements**, including information about requirements needed by applications running in mobile terminals to achieve a certain service quality for end users, such as end-to-end delay for real-time chatting application, jitter for on-line video streaming service, throughput for content distribution system.
- **User Preferences**, including subjective information about the extent of satisfaction for end users, such as service quality expectations, economic concerns, energy efficiency consideration.

Note that in different decision-making algorithms, different sets of the above parameters are provided to satisfying different requirements for both stability and accuracy concerns. For instance, some parameters are time-variant in nature, such as received signal strength or the available bandwidth, while other parameters are static or much stabler in a long term, such as the technology type and average network load. Accuracy plays an important role in collecting those parameters to obtain final decision results. It needs more overhead to collect more accurate data and improve the quality, such as more signaling exchanges in handover protocols. Therefore, there exists a tradeoff between accuracy and overhead in designing handover decision algorithms.

In addition, collection approaches for such network information are also different in different handover architectures and protocols. For example, in a mobile-controlled handover system, mobile clients can collect the required information only in the terminal side. Specifically, the network conditions in WLANs, such as security levels, available bandwidth and signal quality, can be obtained from beacon frames according to the IEEE 802.11 standards. Besides from information acquisition from direct network measurements, parameter prediction provides another common approach to obtain network conditions based on recent states or history data. For example, the average network load per day can be easily predicted according to the history measurements from a long period.

3.1.2.2 Decision Making

After decision criteria are set, handover decision-making algorithms should be invoked to find the best target network at any time anywhere, especially for current dual-mode or multi-mode terminals. This capability is called *Always Best Connected* (ABC) in wireless communication systems. With the support of ABC, terminals can always find the best wireless access networks according to their different QoS requirements or personal preferences. Telecommunication operators can also benefit. For example, according to the decision-making strategies, network operators could analyze the distribution of mobile data and deploy the appropriate number of Wi-Fi access points to offload the data from cellular networks.

In the following, we summarize the decision-making models widely used in network selection, including

- **Utility Function Model**
  The utility is represented as the quality level that a communication service provides to the decision maker. Different mobile users with different applications may have different utility functions according to their own benchmarks for on-going services. In general, utilities can be categorized into monotony and non-monotony. If the perceived service quality shows a monotonic increase and decrease with the associated attributes, the utility is regarded as monotonic utility, such as signal strength, delay, packet loss. It's worth noting that in real practice, the best value of monotonic utilities may not be chosen as the final decision due to economic or overhead concerns. For example, the value closest to application demands is preferred.
- **Multiple-Attribute-Decision-Making Model**
  A final decision is determined among the available alternatives that are presented by multiple attributes. In general, MADM algorithms adopted in network selection can be classified into compensatory and non-compensatory algorithms. In the non-compensatory algorithms, acceptable alternatives are chosen to meet the minimum requirements, while in compensatory algorithms, multiple attributes are combined to select the best solution.
- **Combinational-Optimization Model**
  The decision-making problem is formulated as some classic combinatorial optimization problems, such as knapsack and bin packing problems, to find an optimum solution in a finite solution space. For example, in a network selection mapping to a knapsack problem, mobile terminals and networks are regarded as items and knapsacks, respectively. Resource constraints of a network, such as bandwidth and number of concurrent users, are mapping to the capacity of a knapsack. Access cost to networks and utility for terminals stand for the cost and the profit of an item in a knapsack. After formulation, the network selection problem can be solved by the approaches to classic knapsack problems.
- **Game-Theory Model**
  The decision-making process is considered as a cooperative or non-cooperative game between different players involved in handover procedures and find the

equilibrium of the game system by providing best strategy for each player. A comprehensive survey on game theory application in handover decision is recently provided by Ramona Trestian et al. in [10]. In that survey, game-theory based approaches are firstly classified into three major categories according to players participating the network selection games, including User-vs.-User, User-vs.-Networks and Networks-vs.-Networks approaches. In each category, both game types, non-cooperative and cooperative games, exist according to the different natures of network entities involved in handover decision.

It's worth mentioning that different models have different features, such as objective and centralization of execution. Network performance in terms of complexity, speed and precision is also different. It is possible that two or more approaches are combined together to retain all benefits and form an integrated approach. A survey on mathematical modeling for network selection in heterogeneous wireless networks can be found in [11], which the reader is referred to for more details.

3.1.3 Handover Execution

After the handover decision is made, a connection is required to be set up to the target candidate network, which is the output of the handover decision. If there is a connection between MN and the original network, a handover is executed to tear down the existing connection and forward the re-routed data to the new connection. Details of handover execution depend greatly on the inter-networking models. There are two mainstream models for inter-networking in heterogeneous wireless networks, Generic Access Network (GAN) [2] and I-WLAN [1].

The objective of GAN is to extend circuit-switching and packet-switching services of cellular networks to a variety of IP broadband access networks. GAN model is not limited to the IEEE 802.11 network, but the integration of cellular networks and IEEE 802.11 networks is the widely used scenario in GAN. Figure 3.2 shows the functional architecture of the GAN model, where GANC is the control gateway for non-cellular networks. Since the GAN model treats non-cellular networks as part of cellular networks, the dual-mode mobile terminal has to be modified in the low-layer protocols, such as embedding the 3GPP protocol into the IEEE 802.11 stack to achieve unified management in both networks.

Since GAN is a tightly coupled model, the handover decision is initiated and implemented by the network-side. The handover process of MT from cellular networks to GAN is shown in Fig. 3.3. Taking IEEE 802.11 network as an example, MT needs to associate with the target AP, establish a secure tunnel using EAP-SIM and IKEv2, and then get authenticated. After that, it needs to obtain a local address in IEEE 802.11 network, and use the local address to establish a secure tunnel with GANC to get the address in the cellular network. It is a soft handover from cellular networks to IEEE 802.11 network.

The handover process of MT from GAN to cellular networks is shown in Fig. 3.4. Since the IEEE 802.11 networks may disconnect at any time, the handover

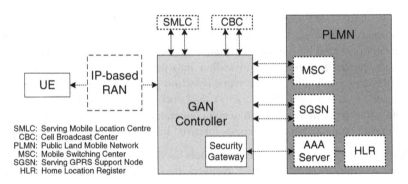

Fig. 3.2 GAN functional architecture (Reprinted from [2])

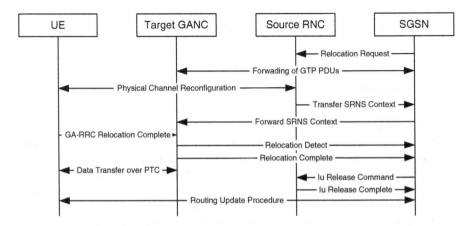

Fig. 3.3 Handover from cellular networks to GAN (Reprinted from [2])

process may suffer from short-term packet loss and delay. Handover within IEEE 802.11 networks controlled by a GANC adopts the EAP-SIM fast re-authentication mechanisms. However, these kinds of mechanisms still incur significant handover latency.

The objective of I-WLAN is to integrate 3GPP networks and IEEE 802.11 WLAN network on top of PS service layer. The I-WLAN interworking network model is shown in Fig. 3.5. Similar to the GAN, a special gateway PDG is responsible for access control from WLAN to 3GPP networks. MT can only connect to the Internet through the WLAN network, rather than to 3GPP networks, where AAA servers in 3GPP networks only provide MT the authentication service in WLAN.

Moreover, the dual-mode terminal does not need to be modified in the protocol layer, because the IEEE 802.11 network and 3GPP network protocol stacks are independent. MT obtains access to the 3GPP network following a standard process, and connects to the WLAN based on EAP-SIM or EAP-AKA and the IKEv2.

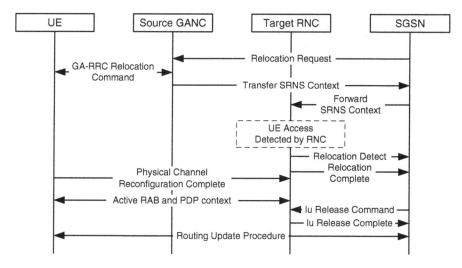

Fig. 3.4 Handover from GAN to cellular networks (Reprinted from [2])

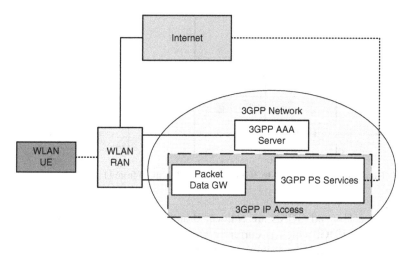

Fig. 3.5 I-WLAN inter-networking model (Reprinted from [1])

If the MT connects only to the Internet, it only needs to finish the authentication by EAP-SIM or EAP-AKA. However, if the MT accesses 3GPP networks, it needs to establish a secure tunnel with the PDG after finishing the first authentication phase by EAP-SIM or EAP-AKA.

Since I-WLAN is a loosely coupled model, the handover decision is initiated and implemented by the MT. For handover from 3GPP networks to I-WLAN, MT executes the handover, as shown in Fig. 3.6, which adopts Mobile IP in its mobility

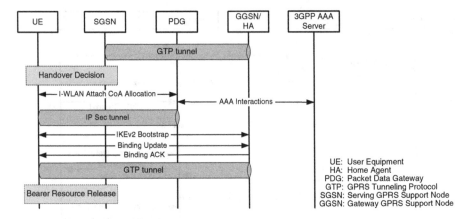

Fig. 3.6 Handover from 3GPP networks to I-WLAN (Reprinted from [1])

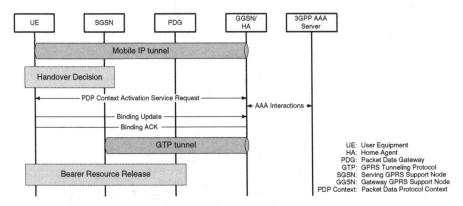

Fig. 3.7 Handover from I-WLAN to 3GPP networks (Reprinted from [1])

management. HA and GGSN are collocated and the CoA of MT in WLAN is the address of the PDG, which is currently associated with UE. PDG forwards data packets to MT through the secure tunnel established using the local address of MT in WLAN. Handover from 3GPP networks to I-WLAN is a soft handover and the connection in 3GPP network is not lost until access to I-WLAN is complete.

The handover process of MT from I-WLAN to 3GPP networks is shown in Fig. 3.7. Similar to the handover procedure from GAN to cellular network, it may also involve short-term packet loss and delay, due to the disconnection in WLAN. Handover within IEEE 802.11 networks controlled by a GANC adopts the EAP-SIM fast re-authentication mechanisms. However, these kinds of mechanisms still incur significant handover latency.

3.2 Mobility Management

Handover management focuses on the procedure to conduct handovers between two networks, while mobility management is much more general, and addresses the entire solution to maintain communications while users are mobile.

3.2.1 Network-Layer Mobility Support

In current all-IP based networks, an IP address is the unique identification for a host on the Internet. Data packets are also routed to specific destinations based on IP addresses. When a mobile node moves from one network to another, its IP address may be changed due to the different network configurations. In order to enable the mobile terminal to receive packages correctly after movement, network-layer mobility management protocols should be executed to maintain the on-going traffic flows.

Mobile IP is a common solution to solve this problem by redirecting packages from the home of a mobile node to its current location. In general, Mobile IP has three main functional entities, namely Mobile Node (MN), Home Agent (HA) and Foreign Agent (FA). MN is a mobile terminal, which changes its Point of Attachments (PoA) and attempts to maintain communication connections after handover completion. HA is a functional entity in the home network of MN, which maintains the updated location information of MN and redirects the data flows destined to MN through the Care-of-Address (CoA). FA is another functional entity in the foreign network, which assigns a CoA to MN when MN is registered and provides routing services to MN.

Mobile IP supports mobility management through the following steps:

- **Agent Discovery**
  An MN is able to determine when it has moved from one network to another, and whether the network is the node's home or a foreign network. This can be achieved by receiving and resolving periodical Agent Advertisement messages from each mobility agent. An MN can also obtain the CoA assigned by FA in foreign networks. In addition, an MN can send Agent Solicitation messages to check the availability of nearby mobility agents in the current network.
- **Registration**
  When an MN is in a foreign network, it needs to obtain a care-of address (CoA). This CoA can be obtained by waiting for FA assignment via advertisements, or interacting via Dynamic Host Configuration Protocol (DHCP) or Point-to-Point Protocol (PPP). The HA of the MN needs to update the address binding with the new CoA after the MN registers the CoA with its HA.
- **Routing and Tunneling**
  Mobility agents are responsible for forwarding packets from the home network to the visiting network through a tunnel. The HA encapsulates data packets destined

to MN and tunnels them to the MN's CoA. After capturing the encapsulated packets at the serving FA in the visiting network, FA decapsulates the packets with the MN's CoA and forwards them to MN. The traffic flow is shown in Fig. 3.8.

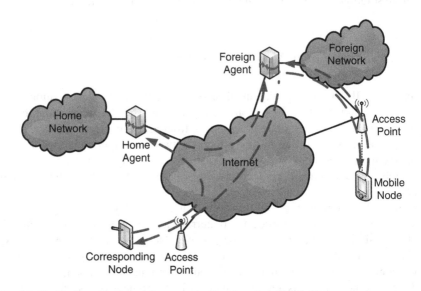

Fig. 3.8 Traffic flow of end-to-end communications based on Mobile IP

The biggest problem of Mobile IP (v4) is triangular routing: MN sends packets to CN directly, but the packets sent by CN need to reach the HA first, then be forwarded to the MN. Route optimization is proposed to solve the triangular routing problem by letting CN send packets directly to the MN through location bindings in the CN. Triangular routing does not exist in Mobile IPv6, because every node has the MN entity and is able to do route optimization, but for Mobile IPv4, normal mobile nodes do not run the MN entity of Mobile IP, and those CNs cannot do route optimization.

3.2.2 Transport-Layer Mobility Support

The biggest benefit from transport-layer mobility protocols is that changes of network address configurations in different networks are all masked on top of the network layer. Most protocols and applications are compatible with the mobility-enabled transport layer, and can easily be ported to such a network environment. Mobile SCTP (mSCTP) is one such protocol to achieve seamless mobility in heterogeneous wireless networks. mSCTP [8] is based on the new generation of transport layer protocol, Stream Control Transmission Protocol (SCTP) [6], with the extension of Dynamic Address Reconfiguration (DAR) [7]. There are two features in DAR, including multi-homing support and dynamic IP-address manipulation.

- **Multi-homing support**

  An SCTP endpoint is configured as a set of SCTP transport addresses, one of which is a map of an IP address and a port number, with the same port number. So, an SCTP endpoint can use multiple IP addresses to establish a connection with another mSCTP endpoint, which can also be regarded as a connection consisting of different paths between the two endpoints. In default configuration, only one path is used to forward the data flow, which is called the primary path with a primary IP address.

- **Dynamic IP-address Manipulation**

  An SCTP endpoint can add and delete its IP address during the connection period to another endpoint. In addition, an SCTP endpoint can also be capable of informing the other endpoint of the ongoing connection between the current primary path and IP address.

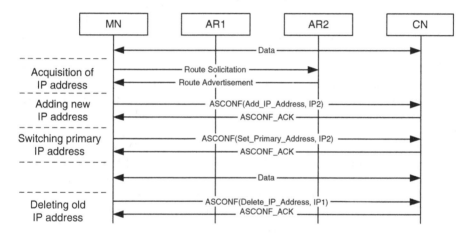

Fig. 3.9 Signaling flow of mSCTP-based handover (Reprinted from [8])

mSCTP follows four steps to achieve seamless handover, and the signaling flow of mSCTP-handover is illustrated in Fig. 3.9.

Step 1: Acquiring an IP address in the new network.

In the overlapping area covered by current and target networks, the mobile terminal firstly obtains a new IP address in the target network.

Step 2: Adding the new IP address in SCTP address mapping.

The mobile terminal informs the other endpoint of SCTP connection, to add the new IP address in SCTP address mapping through the message exchanges of *ASCONF* and *ASCONF-ACK* with the parameter of *Add IP Address*.

Step 3: Switching the primary IP address.

The mobile terminal informs the other endpoint of SCTP connection to switch the primary IP address to the new IP address through the message exchanges of *ASCONF* and *ASCONF-ACK* with the parameter of *Set Primary IP Address*.

Step 4: Deleting the old IP address in SCTP address mapping.

The mobile terminal informs the other endpoint of SCTP connection to delete the old IP address in SCTP address mapping through the message exchanges of *ASCONF* and *ASCONF-ACK* with the parameter of *Delete IP Address*.

3.2.3 Application-Layer Mobility Support

The basic idea of application-layer mobility management is that registration control mechanism and handover management are implemented in the application layer. The benefits of such a protocol design include flexibility on service requirements and scalability on system infrastructure. There are two mainstream mobility management protocols in the application layer, namely the Session Initial Protocol (SIP) initiated by IETF and H.323 (Packet-based multimedia communications systems) proposed by ITU-T. In this section, we briefly introduce the SIP protocol [5]. For the information of H.323, we refer the reader to the ITU's standard [9].

In standard operations of SIP calling, both end users have to register with their own SIP registration servers and obtain Uniform Resource Identifiers (URIs) as their subscriber identifications from the servers. After that, end users can initialize SIP requests and proceed the subsequent operations. The call flow of SIP is shown in Fig. 3.10.

User A starts a SIP call request to user B by sending a *INVITE* message with the URI of user B to the local SIP Proxy server. The local SIP Proxy server will forward the request to the remote SIP Proxy server of user B and reply with a *Trying* message. The remote proxy will continue forwarding the request to user B and will reply to the local proxy server with a *Trying* message. Once receiving the *INVITE* message, user B will reply to the remote Proxy server with a *Ringing* message, which is forwarded back to user A. If user B answers the ringing call, a *OK* message will be generated and forwarded to user A, who will respond with a *ACK* message. After that, the call session is established and maintained until the termination with a *Bye* message is generated.

In addition, the SIP protocol defines one common SIP handover scenario, called Mid-call mobility, where a mobile node takes handover to a new network during the call session. After switching a point of attachment and entering a new network, a mobile node first handles all ongoing sessions, and sends the new INVITE request to the correspondence node directly. In the new INVITE message, the session ID should be kept the same as the previous one, and the Contact field should be filled in with the new IP address. Finally, the mobile node needs to register its new IP address to the home SIP server to update the address binding. The signaling flow of SIP mid-call handover is shown in Fig. 3.11.

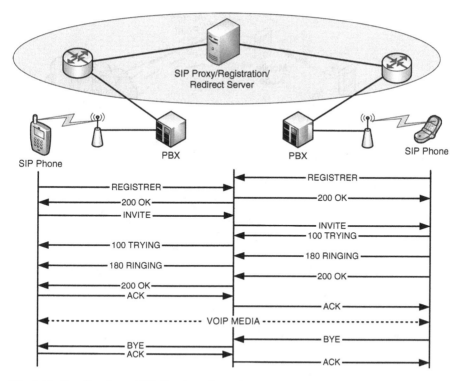

Fig. 3.10 Signaling flow of SIP (Reprinted from [5])

3.3 Case Studies in HAWK Platform

3.3.1 HAWK Platform

As the next generation mobile wireless networks are based on all-IP networks, all kinds of advanced wireless access technologies such as 3G, beyond 3G cellular networks, WLANs and WMNs, will provide users with higher data rates and greater coverage to access the Internet. **HAWK** [3], abbreviated from Heterogeneous Advanced Wireless networKs, was proposed to realize seamless mobility and communication when mobile clients roam among different wireless access networks, which was supported by the Innovation and Technology Fund of the HKSAR government (Fig. 3.12).

In the system scenario, WMN was considered as home network and the other two networks, 3G cellular network and WLAN, as foreign networks for mobile clients. Since we cannot deploy any Mobile IP entity in the foreign networks for administrative reasons, we had to adopt a loosely coupled interworking architecture to support the capability of seamless roaming and non-interrupted communications while mobile client moving in heterogeneous wireless networks. We deployed a

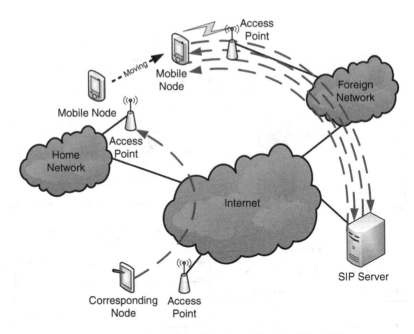

Fig. 3.11 Signaling flow of SIP-based mid-call handover (Reprinted from [5])

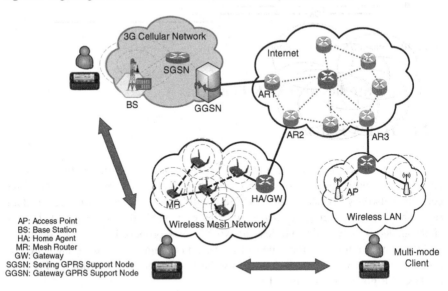

Fig. 3.12 System scenario of HAWK platform

home agent on a mesh gateway in WMN, which we can operate directly. In the foreign networks, we adopted a co-located CoA mode of Mobile IP protocol to treat the foreign networks transparent to mobile terminals. Moreover, some optimization algorithms and roaming protocols were also developed and implemented to support fast and seamless handover in both intra-mesh and inter-networks scenarios.

In this project, we developed two generations of wireless mesh routers, called **T902** mesh router (Fig. 3.13a) and **T903** mesh router (Fig. 3.13b), which both support multi-radio multi-channel capability and seamless roaming functionality. Some of the mesh routers were also deployed in the PolyU campus, as shown in Fig. 3.13c, d, for long-term performance testing and Internet access services.

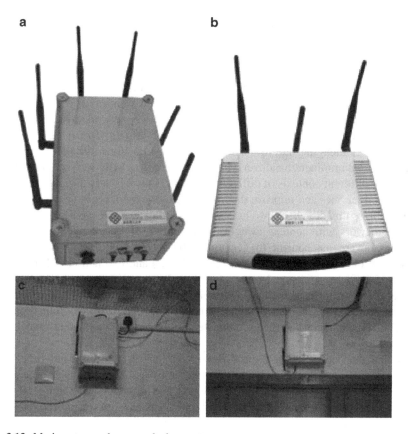

Fig. 3.13 Mesh routers and campus deployment

3.3.2 Context-Aware MIH Framework

3.3.2.1 Introduction

As already mentioned in Sect. 2.3, there are three types of services defined in IEEE 802.21 MIH standard, namely MIES, MICS and MIIS. These services play

Table 3.1 Summary of notations

Notations	Definitions
h_n	Actual handover preparation time of the n_{th} handover
h'_n	Preliminary eHPT of the n_{th} handover
$\hbar_n$	Final eHPT of the n_{th} handover
T_n	Valid history vector for estimation
p_n	Data loss ratio of the n_{th} handover
e_n	Error of between actual time and estimation
d_n	Bias to adjust the output
l, m	Control parameters to adjust bias d_n

important roles in information exchange between different network layers and heterogenous media to provide a standard mechanism to facilitate a fast handover. Among the three services, MIES generates notification events and helps upper layer applications being aware of the status change from lower network layer. As the only prediction event in all event services, MIH $Link\_Going\_Down$ (LGD) event is the most challenging one to handle in MIES, which aims to notify the user to prepare for the imminent handover. However, the unified MIH services are not able to identify different contexts of different users, and thus it is very difficult to provide customized services and improve the individual user experience.

To address this drawback, we have proposed to extend the event services in the MIH framework with context-awareness capability [12]. Specifically, we proposed a context-aware mechanism to generate MIH LGD event, which is based on Estimation of Handover Preparation Time ($eHPT$) and Estimation of Link Down Time ($eLDT$) from physical-layer switching. When $eHPT$ is equal to $eLDT$, a MIH LDG event is generated. Different from existing works, which focus on the fixed settings on thresholds signal strength from physical layer, our proposed mechanism guarantees that the pre-allocated time for users is sufficient to make the final handover.

In this mechanism, two impact factors on handover preparation time were taken into consideration. One is the time caused by essential handover procedures defined in handover management algorithms and protocols, including message passing, timeout settings, etc. The other one is packet loss ratio for on-going links, which affects the time for successful message exchange. We collected historical HPT from the MIH framework as one of our contexts, by which we can estimate the preparation time for the next handover without knowing the details of handover procedures. Furthermore, our proposed module can dynamically adjust the estimation time by detecting the real-time network packet loss ratio. As a result, the estimated handover preparation closely matches users' actual requirements. To simplify the presentation, we list key parameters in Table 3.1.

3.3.2.2   Extended MIH Framework with Context-Awareness Module

The time to trigger a handover does not only depend on the LDT, but is also related to the actual HPT of different users. The lower layer estimates the residual LDT by measuring the signal strength, and periodically reports the estimation to the MIH framework through MIH SAP interfaces. In order to generate a timely MIH LGD event for handover procedures, we developed a context-awareness extension for the original IEEE 802.21 MIH framework. The system architecture of the extended framework is shown in Fig. 3.14. Our context-awareness module calculates $eHPT$ according to historical data and on-going packet loss ratio. When $eHPT$ is going to be less than the estimated residual LDT for the on-going link, a MIH LGD event is generated and forwarded to the upper layer to trigger a handover. Thus, mobile user always has enough time to complete the handover procedure.

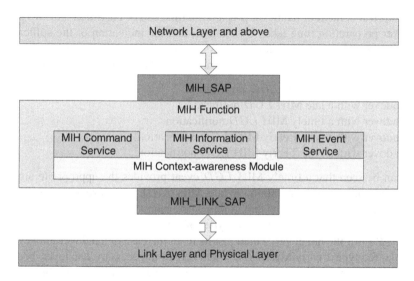

Fig. 3.14   System architecture of CMIH

There are two categories of context information collected by the module, namely historical and current contexts. The historical context included the information related to previous handover, such as historical HPT, while the current context consisted of network statistics related to on-going connections, such as packet loss ratio. The detailed function components in the proposed context-awareness module are shown in Fig. 3.15. The module is comprised of Context Information, Estimator, Adaptor, and Result components. The Context Information part stores historical HPT and collects on-going packet loss ratio. Estimator part conducts the primary estimation based on the above context information part. Adaptor part compares the estimation result made by Estimator and historical context collected in Context Information part. Then, the Result part determines the final decision and completes the whole process.

Fig. 3.15 Working flow of
context-awareness module

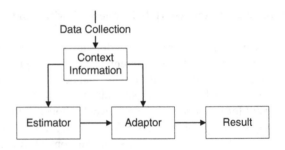

3.3.2.3   Context-Aware Handover Preparation Time Estimation

Historical Context of Handover Preparation Time

The historical context of handover preparation time can be classified into two parts: handover preparation time taken by the user, and the indication of the sufficiency of the last handover preparation time. As shown in Fig. 3.16, we identified five scenarios related to MIH LGD events during a handover procedure, which are

1. Handover without a MIH LGD notification,
2. Handover with a late MIH LGD notification,
3. Handover with a timely MIH LGD notification,
4. Handover with a type 1 early MIH LGD notification,
5. Handover with a type 2 early MIH LGD notification.

It can be seen that a timely MIH LGD event provides the appropriate amount of time for handover preparation. A late MIH LGD event provides insufficient preparation time, which means that mobile node cannot finish the necessary operations before link down. The other two types of early MIH LGD events provide too much HPT for the handover, which results in an increase in handover latency. For example, the type 1 early MIH LGD event causes unnecessary handover, because its handover management directly triggers handover after receiving the MIH LGD event, while the type 2 early MIH LGD event triggers early handover preparation procedure, which may not provide accurate network information for the next handover. If there is no MIH LGD event involved in the handover procedure, mobile terminals have to take the break-before-make manner to initialize a handover.

As shown in Fig. 3.16, the entire handover time consists of three parts, namely handover preparation time h, MIH scanning time t_s, and handover execution time t_e. We assumed that most of the preparation operations involves message exchange on network layer, such as neighbor discovery and context collection, which are almost done before link down. For second part, MIH scanning can be processed before or after link down, depending on the current handover management. Since scanning operation may interrupt on-going communications, MIH scanning is set to be executed before link down in our solution to reduce the service interruption time. However, conducting MIH scanning too early also affects the current connections and still incurs more service interruption time. Therefore, we conducted the MIH scanning before link down within a very short time in the proposed mechanism, by adding a protection interval Δt.

In our context-awareness module, we collected h_n and c_n as the user handover preparation time history. They are defined in Eq. 3.1.

$$\begin{aligned} h_n &= t_{MIH\_scan} - t_{Link\_going\_down} \\ c_n &= t_{Link\_down} - t_{MIH\_scan} \end{aligned} \tag{3.1}$$

where h_n denotes the real handover preparation time at round n, and c_n is the value to evaluate whether h_n is sufficient. t_{MIH_scan}, $t_{Link\_going\_down}$ and t_{Link_down} are the system time when the context-awareness module receives these respective commands and events.

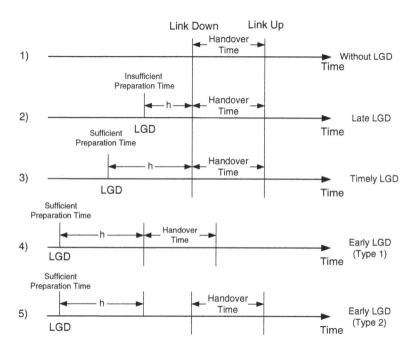

Fig. 3.16 Five handover scenarios related to MIH LGD events

Estimation on Handover Preparation Time

The handover preparation time is affected by the inherent handover preparation procedure and external packet loss ratio on communication channels. The inherent handover preparation procedure is determined by the handover management algorithms and protocols. Since the operations are pre-defined by the management mechanisms, the time caused by the handover preparation procedure is relatively stable when the handover management scheme is configured.

On the other hand, external packet loss ratio affects the packet delivery time, and dynamically changes with the time in wireless networks. Griffith et al. [4] investigated the relationship between message transmission time and packet loss ratio via UDP and TCP protocols under the MIH framework. There were some interesting observations in their work. For example, when the packet loss ratio is below 50 %, message transmission time approximately keeps linear with packet loss ratio for both UDP and TCP sessions. If the packet loss ratio is greater than 50 %, the performance will degrade dramatically due to the larger latency. Based on the above investigation, we thus assumed that the threshold of packet loss ratio to trigger a handover is 50 %. If the packet loss ratio is above the threshold, mobile node has to start the handover mechanism to find a better network.

$$R = \frac{\sum x_i t_i - \sum x_i \sum t_i}{\sqrt{\left[\sum x_n^2 - (\sum x_n)^2\right]\left[\sum t_n^2 - (\sum t_n)^2\right]}} \tag{3.2}$$

The preparation time estimation algorithm is shown in Algorithm 1. When there is no historical record, preparation time is set as a pre-defined value. If there is only one historical record, we can only carry out the adaptation function based on prior history and c_n. If c_{n-1} is below zero, which means the previous handover preparation time was insufficient, the historical context is not valid. In such a case, we empty this historical context, and increase m by one to enlarge estimation bias; otherwise, we use the estimation time of previous handover. If there are more than two valid records in a history, we can calculate the linear regression equation. We use c_{n-2} to check whether there are more than two valid histories.

It is important to notice that in this situation, we use the combination of c_{n-1} and regression correlation value R to distinguish whether the handover preparation process has changed. The R is Pearson's correlation coefficient, which is defined in Eq. 3.2. Its value lies between 0 and 1. When R equals to 1, it means the perfect correlation. When R equals 0, it indicates there is no correlation. It is commonly accepted that when R is higher than 0.8, then there is high correlation. The idea behind the combination is to distinguish handover procedure changes and abnormal data collected with the same handover procedure. If the process has changed, then there is no need to use historical context, so we empty old history. Finally, is returned as the result after time estimation and adaptation.

Algorithm 2 describes the $update$ routine for parameter h'_n, e_n and d_n. We adopt linear regression function to analyze the handover preparation time and packet loss ratio, and make estimation for h'_n. In order to approach the real value of h, we calculate the error e_n between the result of preparation time in our regression equation, and the real historical record in our context-awareness module. To adaptively make modifications and follow the current situation, we implement adaption parameter d_n, which comprises two adaptation parts. The first adaptation part is based on the previous handover preparation error, and the latest two-time packet loss ratio. The second part provides some extra time Δt to distinguish early and right MIH LGD events. In addition, if a late MIH LGD event occurs, parameter l and m can add much more additional time into this adaptation. It increases the adaptation speed to fit large user handover preparation time requirement changes.

Algorithm 1 Algorithm for handover preparation time estimation

---

INPUT: $l, \Delta t, h'_{n-1}, T = \{T_0, T_1, \ldots, T_{n-1}\}$
OUTPUT: p_n

  1: $K = |T|$
  2: **if** $K == 0$ **then**
  3:    $\hbar_n = default\ time$
  4: **else if** $K == 1$ **then**
  5:    **if** $c_{n-1} \leqslant 0$ **then**
  6:       $m + +\ and\ empty(T)$;
  7:    **end if**
  8:    $update() \rightarrow h'_n, e_{n-1}, d_n; \hbar_n = h_{n-1} + d_n$
  9: **else if** $K \geqslant 2$ **then**
10:    **if** $c_{n-1} \leqslant 0$ **then**
11:       **if** $R < 0.8$ **then**
12:          $m + +; empty(T)$;
13:       **end if**
14:       $update() \rightarrow h'_n, e_{n-1}, d_n; \hbar_n = h_{n-1} + d_n$
15:    **else**
16:       **if** $c_{n-2} < 0$ **then**
17:          $update() \rightarrow h'_n, e_{n-1}, d_n; \hbar_n = h_{n-1} + d_n$
18:          $delete\ T_{n-2}$
19:       **else**
20:          $update() \rightarrow h'_n, e_{n-1}, d_n; \hbar_n = h'_n + d_n$
21:          $m = 0$;
22:       **end if**
23:    **end if**
24: **end if**
25: **return** $\hbar_n$

Algorithm 2 Algorithm for *update()* routine

INPUT: $l, \Delta t, h'_{n-1}, T = \{T_0, T_1, \ldots, T_{n-1}\}$
OUTPUT: h'_n, e_{n-1}, d_n

  1: $\tilde{a} = \frac{\sum_{i=0}^{n}(p_i - \tilde{p})(h_i - \tilde{h})}{\sum_{i=0}^{n}(p_i - \tilde{p})^2}$
  2: $\tilde{b} = \tilde{h} - \tilde{a} \times \tilde{p}$
  3: $h'_n = \tilde{a} \times p_n + \tilde{b}$
  4: $e_{n-1} = h_{n-1} - h'_{n-1}$
  5: $d_n = e_{n-1} \times p_n / p_{n-1} + \Delta t \times l^m$

3.3.2.4 Performance Evaluation

In this section, we conducted simulation-based experiments to evaluate the performance of context-aware estimation to handoff preparation time for MIH *LGD* event. In order to predict the change of signal strength of wireless networks, a prediction algorithm in [13] was adopted in our framework.

We set up a homogeneous WLAN test-bed with three APs and developed MIIS in a Lenovo Thinkpad T61 notebook. In addition, we implemented basic services of MIH to facilitate the complete handover process, including handover preparation and execution. A prototype of MIH platform with context awareness extension has been developed in our **HAWK** platform, which currently supports the core features of the IEEE 802.21 standard.

Experiment Settings

We evaluated our context-aware time estimation in three situations. The first one has a fixed handover preparation procedure with changing packet loss ratio. The second one has both changes in handover procedure and packet loss ratio. To clearly show the adaptation of our context-awareness, the handover procedure only changes once. The third one compares our context-aware time estimation with three predefined and static handover preparation times for a fixed handover preparation procedure. We test all handover procedures with an initiate handover preparation time estimation of 250 ms, and set l as 5, and Δh as 50 ms.

We considered two types of handover procedures, as shown in Fig. 3.17. The type 1 handover procedure called the $MIH_Get_Information_Request$ to get neighbor information from the MIH server database, then called MIH candidate query command to obtain more real time and specific information, while the type 2 handover procedure only called $MIH_Get_Information_Request$.

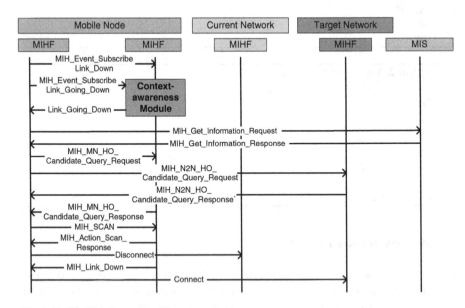

Fig. 3.17 Working flow of handover procedure

Evaluation Results

A comparison of handover time of different types is represented in Fig. 3.18, including type 1 handover, type 2 handover and an adaptation mode with context-awareness capability. If there is no context-awareness mechanism, more early MIH LGD events may be generated to trigger unnecessary handovers in type 1 handover, while more time will be caused due to the inaccurate handover information in type 2 handover.

As shown in Fig. 3.18, since the actual time is in a time-varying nature, it is very difficulty to find a pre-defined value to fit all the scenarios during the users' movement. When the context-awareness mechanism was adopted in the handover management, the estimation time with the adaptation mode closely follows the actual time used in the handover procedures, which means our proposed module could adapt the changing network conditions and provide a timely event for the handover decision. It is worth mentioning that most of estimations of HPT are a little greater than the actual time. This is because we added a protection factor Δt to the HPT in calculating the final $eHPT$, to avoid the effect of estimation error. In doing so, we can guarantee that there is always sufficient HPT provided to mobile users to finish the handover.

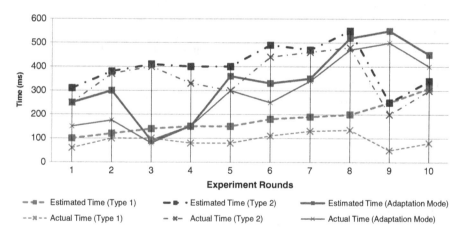

Fig. 3.18 Performance of time estimation for handover preparation

In addition, the relationship between handover preparation time and number of handovers was identified by field testing. We set different values of handover preparation time and logged the trace of users' movement along a corridor in PolyU campus. As shown in Table 3.2, we found that greater handover preparation time incurred more handovers. It is because that the handover context is outdated if the HPT is too large to collect the accurate network statistics. Therefore, the proposed context-awareness module can provide sufficient but not too large preparation time by adapting a protection factor Δt in final calculation.

Table 3.2 Relationship between handover preparation time and number of handovers

Handover preparation time	Number of handovers
200 ms (fixed setting)	20
400 ms (fixed setting)	26
800 ms (fixed setting)	36
Adaptive time with context-aware estimation	18

3.3.3 UMIP: UDP-Tunnel Based Mobile IP

3.3.3.1 Introduction

In order to support seamless communication and mobility support in our **HAWK** platform, we adopted a loosely coupled interworking architecture with Mobile IP to achieve location management and handover management. In this architecture, we implemented a lightweight mobile IP protocol, called UMIP (UDP-tunnel based Mobile IP) to facilitate the integration of different networks in **HAWK** platform.

The major challenges in the implementation of UMIP is to solve the following two practical issues in our platform. One is how to treat foreign networks transparent to end users, and in our implementation UMIP adopts a co-CoA (co-located Care-of Address) mode, in which FA entities are excluded from the protocol operations. The other one is how to handle different addressing schemes in different networks, and UMIP implements a novel UDP-tunnel management mechanism and NAT traversal technologies. In doing so, UMIP supports both public and private foreign IP addresses in foreign networks, and also supports both public and private home addresses (HoA) in home networks.

3.3.3.2 Protocol Framework

In this section, we present the main components of the protocol framework of UMIP, including MN Registration/Online, MN Handover, MN Offline. After that, the message format used in UMIP is illustrated. To simplify the following presentation, we list the notations and abbreviations in Table 3.3.

MN Registration/Online

The signaling flow of the process that a MN inside a private network completes a registration to its HA in a public network is shown in Fig. 3.19. In the beginning, the MN is assigned to a private IP address of 192.168.0.2 via DHCP service in a foreign private network and the HA is located in a home public network with a public IP address 158.132.10.174.

Table 3.3 Notations and abbreviations

Notations	Definitions
HA	Home Agent
MN	Mobile Node
RP	Registration Port, UDP port number for registration
ATP	Assigned Tunnel Port, UDP port number for tunnel data transmission
VND	Virtual Network Driver, a virtual interface to read and write IP packages. In MN, it's used as the default route entry interface, and in HA, it's used as the host route entry interface for the MN
Reg	Registration message
RegRply	Registration Reply message
TM	Tunnel Management message
KA	Keep Alive, one type of TM. It will periodically be sent by MN if there is no data transmission during a certain interval
T/V	Assigned Tunnel Port and VND pair for a MN

The registration procedure is detailed as follows:

Step 1: MN assign a T/V pair for itself, sends a Reg to HA with its HoA using its current network connection.

Step 2: HA receives the Reg, and assign a T/V pair for the MN, HA sends back a RegRply with the ATP to the MN.

Step 3: MN receives the RegRply and uses the IPHA + ATP-HA (given by HA carried by RegRply) as its remote address for the tunnel in T/V-MN.

Step 4: T/V-MN (T/V in MN) will send data or periodical KA to the tunnel. Once T/V-HA receives a package from the tunnel, it will use the source address (IP + UDP port) of the received package as its remote address for the tunnel.

A MN-binding is created through the registration, and includes T/V-MN and T/V-HA operations. This binding will be activated/deactivated or modified automatically, according to the MN location. A similar procedure for a MN in public networks but without NAT can be conducted to complete the registration.

MN Handover

To reduce the number of registration in different networks, UMIP implemented a registration-free mechanism to support MN's handover without de-registration. A MN needs to do the registration only at the first time it connects to a network. The network can be a home network or a foreign network. After the first registration, the registration information can be maintained during MN's handover procedures.

Since the main task for UMIP is to support the location management in handover scenarios, the capability to monitor and detect underlying network conditions is

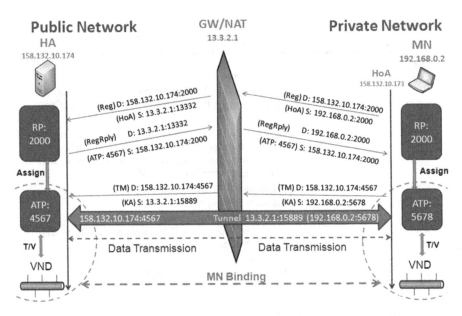

Fig. 3.19 MN registration procedures

not supported by UMIP. So, the low level handover is done by other fast handover modules or software, which should send a trigger information to UMIP module to indicate the completion of network switches. Once a network switch is completed, MN will check the location of current networks:

1. **At home network**-*Deactivation of T/V-MN Module.*
   Once the T/V-HA receives a package from the tunnel and has found that the source IP address is the same as the HoA of the MN, it means the MN is back to home, and it will deactivate the T/V-HA itself.
2. **At foreign network**-*Activation or Reactivation of T/V-MN Module.*
   Once the T/V-HA receives a package from the tunnel and has found that the source IP address is not the same as the HoA of the MN, it means the MN is foreign, it will activate or reactivate (do nothing if the previous network of MN is also foreign) the T/V-HA automatically changes its remote address (equal to the source address of received packages).

In order to speed up the handover, MN will send 3 KAs (with an interval of 25 ms) to the HA right after the activation or deactivation of its T/V-MN to ensure the T/V-HA could receive packages from the new address as soon as possible.

MN Offline

In order to reduce meaningless data transmission after a MN is offline, it is necessary to detect whether a MN is offline and deactivate or destroy the T/V-HA module for it. Since KA messages are always transmitted between T/V-MN and T/V-HA, the existence of KA messages can be a indicator whether a MN is online or offline.

UMIP uses a simple timeout mechanism to detect whether a MN is online or offline. If there is no data or KA messages received from the MN in the corresponding T/V-HA before a timeout fires, the MN will be labeled as offline and the T/V-HA will be deactivated or destroyed (only when current status is deactivated).

Message Format

The packet structure of protocol messages in UMIP is shown in Fig. 3.20. The common message as shown in the top figure includes six fields, among which the first five fields comprise the packet header. For different functional messages, such as registration packets, registration reply packets and data packets, the field of *Message Content* in the common message is formatted by different data structure defined in the other figures.

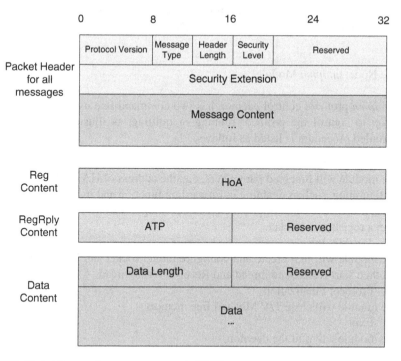

Fig. 3.20 Packet format of common message in UMIP

The detailed description of packet structure is listed as follows.

1. Protocol Version (8 bits): version of the protocol
2. Message Type (4 bits): including Reg, RegRply, Data, TM(such as KA), ...
3. Header Length (4 bits): length of the header, unit in 4 bytes
4. Security Level (4 bits): at most 16 levels, different levels will carry different security extensions. Level 0 means no security extension and the Header Length will be 1.
5. Security Extension (at most 56 bytes): security enhancement for this message/package, the Header Length includes the size.
6. Message Content of different message types:

    (a) Reg: *HoA* is the HoA address for a MN
    (b) RegRply: *ATP* is assigned by HA for the MN
    (c) Data: *Data Length* is the total bytes of the transmitted data
    (d) TM: till now there is only one type of TM, namely KA

3.3.3.3 Implementation Details

Currently, UMIP protocol is implemented in Linux of kernel version above 2.4 with built-in tun module support. The protocol is mainly executed in two network entities, mobile node and home agent. In our implementation, we separated the functions into two parts, namely *umipmn* module and *umipha* module.

Mobile Node: *umipmn* Module

The *umipmn* protocol control daemon has two command-line user interfaces: *start* and *stop* to control the protocol running or quitting, as illustrated in Fig. 3.21. The detailed procedure is listed as follows.

Step 1. Protocol Init
   The module will first read parameters, e.g. the address of HA, and check system configuration, such as enabling ip forwarding function and inserting tun module. Then, it will start data initiation, create a listening thread for location update and open a registration socket.
Step 2. T/V-MN Init
   The module will first create and configure tunnel socket and VND (tun device), and then start Read/Send thread and Receive/Write thread.
Step 3. Protocol Finalization
   The module will close T/V-MN and free memories.
Step 4. Exit
   The module will quit the daemon.
Step 5. Idle
   The module will wait for the location update messages.
Step 6. Location Update
   The module will receive a message which indicates a completed network switch, and the message contains a interface name of current network connection.

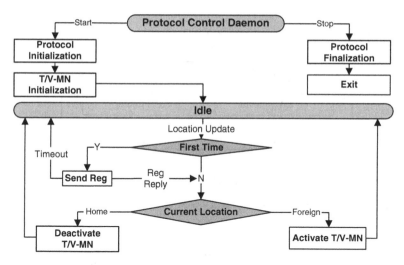

Fig. 3.21 System architecture of umipmn module

Step 7. First time

The module will check whether MN is the first time to do the location update. If yes, it will need to do a registration to the HA.

Step 8. Send Reg

The module will send a Reg to the HA.

Step 9. Timeout

If this module does not receive a RegRply from the HA in 2 s after sending a Reg, that means this registration fails. If it still fails after doing the registration three times, this location update fails.

Step 10. RegRply

After receiving a RegRply which contains the ATP-HA from the HA, the module will update the T/V-MN's remote tunnel address as IPHA + ATP-HA.

Step 11. Location (Home or Foreign)

The module will check the IP address of the interface given by the Location Update message. If it is the same as HoA of the MN, the MN is at home, otherwise the MN is at a foreign network.

Step 12. Deactivate T/V-MN

The module will set the IP of VND interface to NULL and send three KAs to the tunnel.

Step 13. Activate T/V-MN

The module will first add a host route entry for the HA from current route table and replace the default route entry with the VND interface. Then, it will send three KAs to the tunnel.

The work flow of T/V-MN operations illustrated in Fig. 3.22.

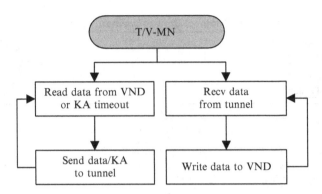

Fig. 3.22 Read/send & receive/write threads of T/V-MN

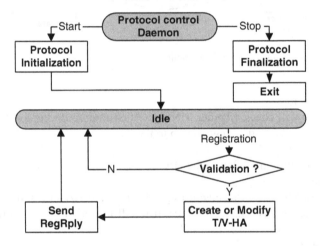

Fig. 3.23 System architecture of umipha module

1. Recv data from tunnel: when received data or KA message from the tunnel, it will automatically change the remote tunnel address to the source address of the received message.
2. Write data to VND: only data will be written to the VND, KA contains no data.

Home Agent: *umipha* Module

The *umipha* protocol control daemon has two command-line user interfaces: *start* and *stop* to control the protocol running or quitting, as shown in Fig. 3.23. The detailed procedure is listed as follows.

Step 1. Protocol Init

The module will first read parameters, e.g. the address of HA, and check system configuration, such as enabling ip forwarding function and inserting tun module. Then, it will start data initiation, create a listening thread for location update and open a registration socket.

Step 2. Protocol Finalization

The module will close T/V-MN and free memories. In addition, this module need to clean ARP entries.

Step 3. Exit

This module will quit the daemon.

Step 4. Idle

This module will wait for Reg messages.

Step 5. Registration

This module will receive a Reg message from a MN.

Step 6. Validation

This module will validate the Reg message adopting different methods for different security levels. For example, in level zero, it is only checked that whether the HoA is in the same subnet with HA.

Step 7. Create or modify T/V-HA

If the corresponding (with the same HoA) T/V-HA does not exist, this module will create a new T/V-HA for the MN. It will activate or deactivate T/V-HA according to the location of MN.

Step 8. Send back RegRply

This module will send a RegRply which contains the ATP of the created or existing T/V-HA back to the MN.

The TV-HA operations control the management of virtual network interface and tunnel, as illustrated in Fig. 3.24.

1. Activate T/V-HA: if the source address of the received message changes to a foreign address (not the HoA), and the previous location of the MN is at home, it will activate the T/V-HA: add a host route entry for the MN to the VND interface.

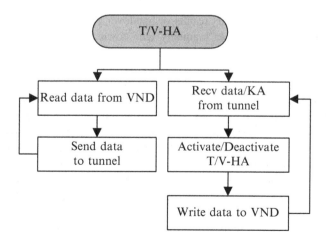

Fig. 3.24 Read/send & receive/write threads of T/V-HA

2. Deactivate T/V-HA: if the source address of the received message changes to the HoA, and the previous location of the MN is at foreign, it will deactivate the T/V-HA: del the host route entry for the MN to the VND interface.
3. Recv data from tunnel: when received a data or KA message from the tunnel, it will automatically change the remote tunnel address to the source address of the received message.
4. Write data to VND: only data will be written to the VND, KA contains no data.

3.3.3.4 Performance Evaluation

We evaluated the handover performance of the UMIP-enabled mobility management in an indoor environment and the handover latency is the main performance indicator to quantify the performance. We set up a mini-testbed based on **HAWK** platform, which consisted of four main entities, including a mobile node, a wireless mesh network, an external WLAN and a commercial 3G network. The detailed configuration of the testing scenario is listed as follows.

1. MN: a notebook with a PCMCIA Wi-Fi network interface card and a 3G HSPA USB modem. The operating system is Ubuntu Linux 8.04 with kernel 2.6.24-16, running *umipmn* module on it. The Wi-Fi card is based on the atheros chips and driven by madwifi 0.94.
2. WMN: two T902 mesh routers, as the home network for the MN, running *umipha* module on it. It assigns a static public home address to the MN.
3. WLAN: a TP-Link WR541G AP, as a foreign network for the MN. It can access the campus Internet and assign a private address to the MN via DHCP when the MN roams into the network coverage.
4. 3G Network: a WCDMA HSPA data network operated in Hong Kong, as a foreign network for the MN. It assigns a private address to the MN via PPP. In this scenario, the 3G network can be considered as a ubiquitous access to the Internet due to its full coverage of the testing field.

In order to collect continuous results of handover performance in such a small scale field, we used a script to manually tear down and bring up some access networks. In doing so, the MN was forced to switch among three networks periodically: $WMN \rightarrow 3G \rightarrow WMN \rightarrow WLAN \rightarrow 3G \rightarrow WLAN \rightarrow WMN$. In this way, the testing logs in six different types of network handover were recorded. In the whole evaluation period, the network switch interval is 10 s and the testing is repeated 50 times. The script will also trigger the *umipmn* module to conduct the Mobile IP registration every time it finishes a network switch.

The entire handover delay is divided into two main part, namely *Connection* delay and *Mobile IP* delay. The *Connection* delay is defined as the period from the time when the MN starts to connect to the time when it is completely connected to a new network, such as IP address acquisition. The *Mobile IP* delay is defined as the period from the time when the *umipmn* module starts to send a registration message to the time when it gets a registration reply. *Connection* delay plus the *Mobile IP*

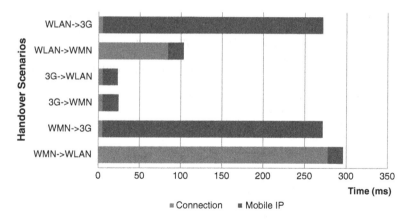

Fig. 3.25 WMN-WLAN-3G handover performance of UMIP

delay is the total handover delay of a network handover. The performance of UMIP can be quantified by the *Mobile IP* delay.

The handover delay results from the above measurements are shown in Fig. 3.25. Among the six types of handover scenarios, it can be easily found that the *Mobile IP* delay in the scenarios from Wi-Fi networks to 3G networks was much greater than the delay in other scenarios. It is mainly because that end-to-end communications always exist long round trip time in 3G networks, which prolong the procedure of signaling exchange.

For the *Connection* delay, handover between Wi-Fi networks took more time to finish the network association, because the only Wi-Fi interface had to conduct break-then-connect paradigm to switch connections. Furthermore, the *Connection* delay from WLAN to WLAN is greater than that from WLAN to WMN. The reason is that the DHCP operations when MN moving into WLAN caused more delay, while, MN obtained the network settings through the static configuration in WMN.

As shown in the figure, the handover delay in UMIP-enabled fast handover was less than 300 ms in worse cases. Through the evaluation, we validated that the UMIP protocol can fully support seamless communication and mobility support in heterogeneous wireless networks.

References

1. 3GPP: Ts 23.234 v6.10.0 3gpp system to wireless local area network (wlan) interworking; system description (release 6) (2006)
2. 3GPP: Ts 43.318 radio access network; generic access network; stage 2 (release 7) (2008)
3. Cao, J., Xie, K., Wu, W., Liu, C., Yao, G., Feng, W., Zou, Y., Wen, J., Zhang, C., Xiao, X., Liu, X., Yan, Y.: Hawk: Real-world implementation of high-performance heterogeneous wireless network for internet access. In: ICDCS Workshops, pp. 214–220 (2009)

4. Griffith, D., Rouil, R., Golmie, N.: Performance metrics for ieee 802.21 media independent handover (mih) signaling. Wirel. Pers. Commun. **52**(3), 537–567 (2010). DOI 10.1007/s11277-008-9629-4. URL http://dx.doi.org/10.1007/s11277-008-9629-4
5. IEEE: Rfc 3261 – sip: Session initiation protocol (2002)
6. IEEE: Rfc 4960 – stream control transmission protocol (2007). URL http://www.ietf.org/rfc/rfc4960.txt
7. IEEE: Rfc 5061 – stream control transmission protocol (sctp) dynamic address reconfiguration (2007). URL http://www.ietf.org/rfc/rfc5061.txt
8. IRTF, I.R.T.F.: Experimental internet-draft: Mobile sctp (2007). URL http://tools.ietf.org/html/draft-riegel-tuexen-mobile-sctp-09
9. ITU-T: H.323: Packet-based multimedia communications systems. URL http://www.itu.int/rec/T-REC-H.323
10. Trestian, R., Ormond, O., Muntean, G.: Game theory: Based network selection: Solutions and challenges. Communications Surveys Tutorials, IEEE **PP**(99), 1–20 (2012). DOI 10.1109/SURV.2012.010912.00081
11. Wang, L., Kuo, G.: Mathematical modeling for network selection in heterogeneous wireless networks: a tutorial. Communications Surveys Tutorials, IEEE **PP**(99), 1–22 (2012). DOI 10.1109/SURV.2012.00044
12. Xiong, M., Cao, J., Zhang, J.: Context-aware mechanism for ieee 802.21 media independent handover. In: Computer Communications and Networks (ICCCN), 2011 Proceedings of 20th International Conference on, pp. 1–6 (2011). DOI 10.1109/ICCCN.2011.6006041
13. Yoo, S.J., Cypher, D., Golmie, N.: Predictive link trigger mechanism for seamless handovers in heterogeneous wireless networks. Wireless Communications and Mobile Computing **9**(5), 685–703 (2009)

Chapter 4
Secure Enhanced Seamless Roaming

In this chapter, we further discuss the security mechanisms to enhance seamless roaming over heterogeneous wireless networks. The existing security solutions in current cellular networks and IEEE 802.11 WLAN are first introduced in Sect. 4.1. Some related work on security-enabled seamless roaming is briefly summarized in Sect. 4.2. Finally, our recent work on secure enhancement in seamless roaming, based on our **SHAWK** platform, is presented in Sect. 4.3, including a unified access test-bed and a VCL/VAS-based security scheme for fast handover.

4.1 Security Mechanisms in Wireless Networks

Security is a fundamental service of mobile network operators and the security requirements should be fulfilled whenever and wherever mobile services are provided. In this section, we take a brief review of the existing security solutions in wireless cellular networks and WLANs.

4.1.1 Security Solutions for Cellular Networks

There are several security requirements that should be considered in the deployment of cellular infrastructure. From the network perspective, the basic requirements for any secure system have to be satisfied in cellular networks, including authentication, integrity and confidentiality. Since core networks in traditional cellular networks are relatively closed only to network operators, we only focus on security issues within wireless access networks in the following part, especially interactions in air interfaces of cellular networks.

J. Cao and C. Zhang, *Seamless and Secure Communications over Heterogeneous Wireless Networks*, SpringerBriefs in Computer Science, DOI 10.1007/978-1-4939-0416-7__4, © The Author(s) 2014

When mobile users want to access the network, the system should identify the right subscribers and authenticate them to use network resources. During communication, the system also needs to guarantee that the information is exchanged without any modification, and that only the destination can view the content. In addition, there are more and more security problems rooted in mobile terminals. For example, the increasing number of smart phones registered on cellular networks has become a large security vulnerability in the existing network infrastructure. First, operating systems in mobile devices are increasingly accessible, in terms of programming capability and controlling, where security holes may be exploited during OS development. Second, when Internet service is prevalent on a mobile platform, the traditional security problems on the Internet migrate to the smart phones, including viruses, malware, rootkits, etc. Apart from the above, mobile users' privacy should be protected in cellular networks. For example, the accurate location information of a cellular subscriber needs to be kept hidden during users' movement.

We take UMTS system as an example to present the specific security mechanisms in cellular networks. UMTS system adopts the UMTS Authentication and Key Agreement (UMTS AKA) protocol to provide mobile users with authentication service using the challenge/response mechanism. Using UMTS AKA protocol, the network and mobile user can be mutually authenticated by each other, and generate a pair of security keys, namely an integrity key (IK) and a cipher key (CK), which are filled into later security operations to guarantee integrity and confidentiality of communication channel and data.

For the integrity requirement, UMTS system implements the UMTS Integrity Algorithm (UIA), also called the F9 algorithm, both in RNC and mobile terminal, as shown in Fig. 4.1. First, the F9 algorithm in the mobile terminal calculates a 32 bit MAC-I value for data integrity using the signaling message as an input parameter, which will be sent to the RNC along with the original signal message. In RNC side, a XMAC-I value is first calculated and then compared to the original MAC-I value. If both are the same, then the integrity of the message has not been compromised.

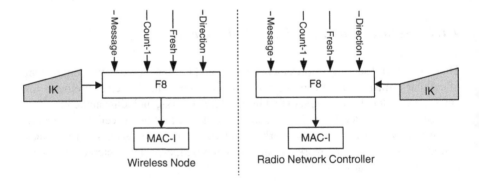

Fig. 4.1 F9 algorithm in UMTS system

For the confidentiality requirement, the F8 algorithm is adopted to protect the signaling message and user data packets, as shown in Fig. 4.2. A mobile terminal first encodes some other information using a CK generated in UMTS AKA protocol. Then, a intermediate result from encoding process is XORed with the data stream bit by bit to get the final cipher stream, which will be transmitted to RNC through the air interface. In RNC side, the same CK and information are used to generate another intermediate stream. Then, the original data stream is obtained by the cipher stream XORed with the latter intermediate stream.

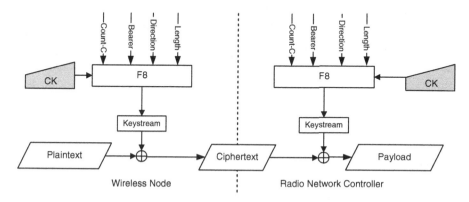

Fig. 4.2 F8 algorithm in UMTS system

4.1.2   Security Solutions for WLAN

The security support for IEEE 802.11 WLAN has been developed in the following chronological order:

• Wired Equivalent Privacy (WEP)
• Wi-Fi Protected Access (WPA)
• IEEE 802.11i (WPA2)

4.1.2.1   Wired Equivalent Privacy

Wired Equivalent Privacy (WEP) is an encryption mechanism introduced as part of the IEEE 802.11-1999 to provide a secure communication for end users in IEEE 802.11 WLAN. WEP adopts RC4 encryption algorithm with different key sizes: 40 bits (WEP-40) , 104 bits (WEP-104) and 232 bits. In addition, 24-bit initialization vector (IV) is added to form the key string for user input. At the transmitter side, the plain text is XORed with the key stream and cipher text is obtained. These steps take place in reverse order at the receiver side using the same key. WEP uses CRC-32 checksum algorithm for data integrity (Fig. 4.3).

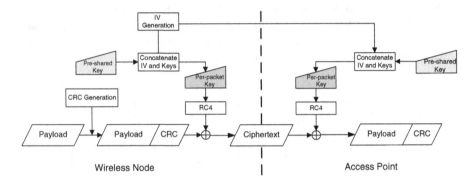

Fig. 4.3 WEP encryption and decryption

Some vulnerabilities in WEP make it crackable. Among them, it is a biggest weakness that the 24-bit IV is usually not long enough to avoid repetition even in a slight traffic-heavy wireless network. Therefore, it is possible to conduct cryptanalysis by sniffing data flows over air interfaces and crack the secure system. In addition, XOR is a simple operation, which can easily be hacked if the other two values are known in the XOR procedure. In practice, WEP cracking can easily be launched using some open source toolkits in minutes [13].

4.1.2.2 Wi-Fi Protected Access

Wi-Fi Protected Access (WPA) can be regarded as an intermediate solution to protect IEEE 802.11 security. Temporal Key Integrity Protocol (TKIP) was adopted as a patch to WEP. As mentioned before, the key used in WEP is manually configured by the network administrator, and the mobile terminal cannot change during the communication. To make it more secure, TKIP dynamically generates a new 128-bit cipher key for each data packet. In order to provide data integrity during transmission, a new algorithm called Michael is used to verify the checksum of the packet. Most of the legacy devices can be upgraded from WEP to WPA through a firmware upgrade. However, WPA still retains some risk of being cracked. For example, Beck-Tews attack can recover the key stream based on an extension of the WEP chop-chop attack [12]. Therefore, after releasing the IEEE 802.11i, IEEE recommended the IEEE 802.11 security mechanism should be upgraded from WEP and WPA to the new solution.

4.1.2.3 IEEE 802.11i

IEEE 802.11i standard (also called WPA2 or RSN, Robust Security Network) was released in June 2004 to enhance the security of WLAN in terms of authentication, integrity and confidentiality. IEEE 802.11i supports two authentication modes. One mode is to authenticate mobile users based on the IEEE 802.1X and EAP protocols (called WPA-Enterprise), and the other one is proposed to use a pre-shared key (called WPA-PSK). After the earlier EAP exchange or WPA-PSK configuration, both sides are provided the shared Pairwise Master Key (PMK), which is used as input on the 4-Way Handshake process to establish robust security network associations between network and wireless stations. The work flow of the 4-Way Handshake is shown in Fig. 4.4.

Fig. 4.4 four-way handshake

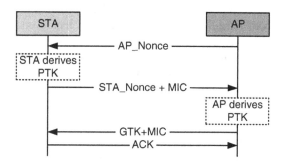

To solve the integrity problem in WLAN, a new algorithm named Michael is used to calculate an 8-byte integrity check called MIC (Message Integrity Code). Michael differs from the old CRC method by protecting both data and the header. Michael implements a frame counter, which helps to protect against replay attacks. To improve data confidentiality, IEEE 802.11i specifies provide two protocols, TKIP and CCMP, with implementation of CCMP being mandatory. TKIP is also adopted in the WPA mechanism, which has been introduced in the previous section. CCMP (Counter with Cipher Block Chaining Message Authentication Code Protocol) is considered the optimal solution for secure data transfer under IEEE 802.11i. CCMP uses AES for encryption. The use of AES requires a hardware upgrade to support the new encryption algorithm.

4.2 Security-Enabled Seamless Roaming

In Chap. 3, we have introduced the related techniques adopted in heterogeneous wireless networks to support seamless mobility for wireless terminals. In order to secure the property and protect the privacy of mobile users, security operations are compulsory in any commercial wireless network. However, the additional enhancement causes signaling operation overhead, which prolongs more handover latency. In this section, we present some related work proposed to optimize security mechanisms in a fast handover process. In general, there are three major categories, namely proactive authentication, context redundancy and optimistic approval.

4.2.1   Proactive Authentication

Proactive authentication is the most important direction to smooth a secure handover in heterogeneous wireless networks. The basic idea of proactive authentication in optimizing security management is to conduct full authentication, or part of the authentication, before mobile terminals move to the new network.

In this category, Media-Independent Pre-Authentication (MPA) framework, which has been approved as RFC 6252 [9], is the prominent solution to support both intra-domain and inter-domain handovers. There are three main functional elements required by the MPA framework in each candidate target network (CTN), called Authentication Agent (AA), Configuration Agent (CA), and Access Router (AR). The AA is responsible for executing the pre-authentication part, and the pre-configuration part is achieved by the other two elements. The signaling flow of MPA is shown in Fig. 4.5

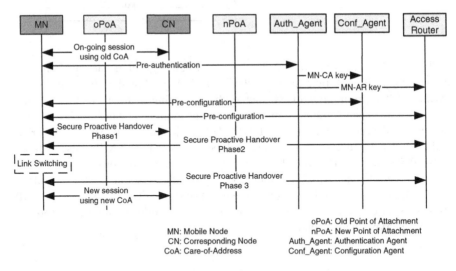

Fig. 4.5 signaling flow of MPA (Reprinted from [9])

The detailed communication flow is described as follows.

1. **Pre-Authentication Phase**
   After discovering a CTN and obtaining the IP addresses of the AA, CA and AR in the CTN, the mobile terminal performs the pre-authentication with the AA to obtain a secure association.

2. **Pre-Configuration Phase**

   After realizing its point of attachment will be changed to a new one, the mobile terminal performs the pre-configuration with the CA to obtain configuration parameters, including the new CoA and AR in CTN. After that, a proactive handover tunnel is established to secure the communication channel between the mobile terminal and AR.

3. **Secure Proactive Handover Phase 1**

   Before the link layer switching, the mobile terminal executes the binding update operations and forwards subsequent data flow to the secure tunnel.

4. **Secure Proactive Handover Phase 2**

   Before completion of the binding update operation, the mobile terminal may delete or disable the secure tunnel and cache the new CoA through the tunnel management protocol.

5. **Link Switching Phase**

   The link layer handover happens in this phase.

6. **Secure Proactive Handover Phase 3**

   After finishing the link switching operation, the mobile terminal immediately assigns the new CoA to the physical interface associated with the new point of attachment.

4.2.2 Context Redundancy

In this category, security-related context is duplicated at a trusted domain, and transferred to the target domain during a handover process. To clearly describe the terms, such as context and context transfer, we refer to RFC 3374 [8] for the standard definitions, which are listed as follows.

- **Context**. The information on the current state of a service required to re-establish the service on a new subnet without having to perform the entire protocol exchange with the mobile host from scratch.
- **Context Transfer**. The movement of context from one router or other network entity to another as a means of re-establishing specific services on a new subnet or collection of subnets.

Specifically, when a mobile user takes a handover to a new domain or network, it first sends a handover request message to the target domain or network. When the message is captured by the target point of attachment and forwarded to the target gateway, the gateway will request the related context from the previous gateway that the user just visited.

The target gateway needs to update the security context in the target point of attachment of the mobile user, once having obtained the requested context. In doing so, the mobile user can be authenticated by the target network without forwarding an authentication request to the mobile user's home network. For example, a context transfer mechanism on AAA protocol was proposed in [7] and a peer-to-peer based context transfer mechanism was designed in [3]. In real implementation, the

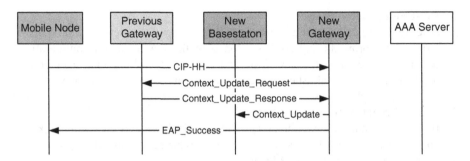

Fig. 4.6 AAA context transfer based on EAP-TLS (Reprinted from [7])

EAP-TLS authentication mechanism is adopted to secure the process of context transfer, which is illustrated in Fig. 4.6.

4.2.3   Optimistic Approval

The third category of security solutions to enhance seamless roaming is optimistic approval, which has two types of re-authentication mechanisms to verify roaming users. One is called strong authentication, and the other is called light-weight authentication. When a mobile user takes handover to a new network, the network adopts the light-weight authentication mechanism to preliminarily verify the user's identity. The credential of such authentication is usually created by another trusted party, such as the previous point of attachment, and distributed through a secure tunnel to both network and client before authentication. In doing so, the latency of the re-authentication can largely be reduced due to an absence of inter-network operations.

After the completion of light-weight authentication, the mobile user is granted optimistic approval to limited network access, such as only keeping ongoing sessions, and is also involved in strong authentication to obtain full privileges to continue using network resources. Obviously, this kind of mechanism strikes a trade-off between security and performance. The implementation of such a security solution can be referred to [2].

4.3 Case Studies in SHAWK Platform

4.3.1 SHAWK Platform

Security issue is one of the most critical concerns in wireless communication systems which is adopted for commercialized use. We have witnessed the growth of conventional communication technologies, such as wireless cellular networks and Wi-Fi based networks, and foresee the coming popularity of ubiquitous Internet access over heterogeneous wireless networks. Security solutions to ubiquitous and seamless Internet access in such network is highly in demand for mobile telecommunication operators. **SHAWK** [4], abbreviated from Secure Heterogeneous Advanced Wireless Networks, was developed to tackle key security problems in providing ubiquitous and seamless Internet access over heterogeneous wireless networks, which was funded by the Innovation and Technology Fund of the HKSAR government (Fig. 4.7).

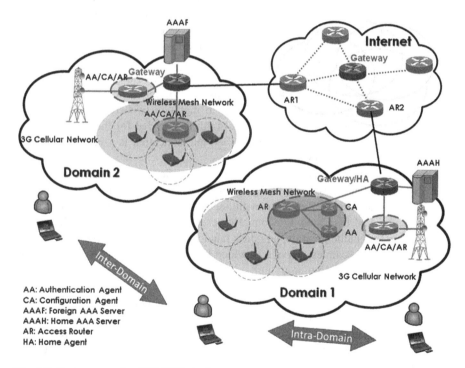

Fig. 4.7 System scenario of SHAWK platform

In this project, we extended our previous **HAWK** project to support security enhancements in pervasive access and seamless handover. We firstly developed secure and seamless handover mechanisms across different wireless networks, which belong to the same or different administrative domains. Then, we developed systematic solutions to secure multi-hop communications and detect possible network attacks in WMNs. Thirdly, we designed mitigation mechanisms to security vulnerabilities during information exchange of security contexts when mobile applications migrate among diversified network infrastructures and various portable devices. Finally, we have implemented and evaluated all the solutions in our **SHAWK** platform, which is upgraded from the previous **HAWK** platform aiming to support seamless roaming over heterogeneous wireless networks.

4.3.2   Unified Access Test-Bead

4.3.2.1   Introduction

3G-WLAN interworking is an emerging technology for the convergence of heterogeneous wireless networks. Solutions to unified authentication using USIM card are an urgent demand for wireless network operators, wireless service providers, and mobile users. However, it is not convenient for a mobile user with a dual-mode device to access 3G-WLAN interworked networks. For example, when a user is using VoIP service and moves from indoors to outside, a handover from WLAN to 3G network will occur and re-authentication should be done to maintain the Internet connection. It is resource-wasting for a wireless network operator or wireless service providers (WSP for short) to maintain two credential items for a single user. So, unified secure access is highly demanded for the integration of heterogeneous wireless networks, and unified authentication is a basic method to achieve unified secure access.

Currently, there are related research works on unified authentication, including USIM-based authentication test-bed [10] for UMTS-WLAN by Korea Electronics and Telecommunications Research Institute, and an initial unified authentication system established by China Telecom. However, they did not consider the issues surrounding fast authentication and fast handover, which are the key problems for ubiquitous and seamless service provided by heterogeneous wireless networks. We aim to establish a ubiquitous unified authentication and secure fast handover platform for the next generation wireless networks on the **SHAWK** platform.

To achieve the goal, we proposed a practical unified authentication scheme in 3G-WLAN interworking [5], which includes a supplicant based on USIM simulator for secure access in the mobile node, an authenticator for forwarding the credentials to the authentication server, and an authentication server based on 3G AuC simulator for generating an authentication vector to verify the supplicant. The 3G AuC simulator is developed for USIM card-based unified authentication. It can support the standard EAP-AKA authentication method for secure access to WLAN access network, and the simplified UMTS-AKA authentication method for secure access to 3G access network. The 3G AuC simulator can respond to the authentication request from a mobile node by executing the UMTS authentication algorithms. Since we are not allowed to modify the commercial 3G network and there is no real 3G access network in our **SHAWK** platform, we used a wired Ethernet connection to simulate 3G secure access.

4.3.2.2   System Architecture and Authentication Mechanisms

In our test-bed, WLAN network and 3G access network were assumed to be operated by the same WSP, and share the same authentication, authorization and accounting server (AS), as shown in Fig. 4.8. The access point (AP) in WLAN is uniquely identified by a basic service set identification (BSSID), and bridges WLAN and wired Internet. It is also the authenticator to relay credentials for MN and AS. The AS is responsible for managing APs, relaying authentication messages to HLR/AuC, and distributing security keys. After successfully being authenticated, the MN can be authorized to attach to the AP for accessing the Internet, and AP will encrypt the data for secure communication in layer 2. The MN can be a smartphone, computer, or other dual-mode equipment with 3GPP and WLAN communication modules.

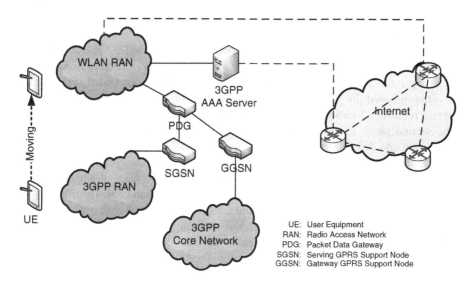

Fig. 4.8 3G-WLAN interworking architecture

The 3G cellular network in the test-bed is a UMTS consisting of access network, including base station and base station controller, core network switching nodes SGSN and core network gateway nodes GGSN for packet-switching, a subscriber information database HLR, an authentication center (AuC) and others. The AuC is often collocated with the HLR, and is responsible for generating an authentication vector for users. They store all users' profiles and related subscription information.

The authentication vector is a 5-tuple composed of a random number RAND, an expected response XRES, a cipher key (CK) for confidentiality protection, an integrity key (IK) and an authentication token (AUTN). Each AV can only be used once between VLR and USIM, and is ordered by the sequence number (SQN).

4.3.2.3   Authentication Mechanisms for Two Types of Network Access

UMTS-AKA for Secure Access to 3G Network

As mentioned in Sect. 4.1, UMTS-AKA is a security protocol used to accomplish the mutual authentication and key agreement based on a long-term pre-shared symmetric key k in USIM card of mobile equipment for secure access to 3G network. Note that secret key k is available only to the AuC in a user's home network. The non-repudiation and non-exposure properties of the pre-installed key with a physical security guarantee is the basis of the security mechanism in such a communication system. The protocol is based on a CHALLENGE/RESPONSE authentication mechanism, which is a security measure intended for mutual verification, without revealing a secret credential shared by the two entities. The key concept is that each entity have to prove to the other that it knows the credential, without actually revealing or transmitting such information.

The process of secure access to a 3G network based on UMTS-AKA authentication mechanism involves three phases. The first phase is connection establishment, including radio attachment and identification by the identity of USIM. This phase is often invoked by a serving network after a first registration of a user, a service request, a location update request, or a connection re-establishment request. The second phase is the main part of the UMTS-AKA process, which includes generation and distribution of authentication vectors (AVs) from the HLR/AuC to VLR/SGSN, authentication based on challenge/response message to confirm each other's legitimacy, and key establishment. AVs include the n set of authentication vectors and can provide n times authentication between MN and SN. The third phase is secure communication by ciphering and integrity protection setup.

In general, after mutual authentication of each other between the USIM and the VLR/SGSN, MN can securely get access to the 3G networks for voice or Internet service.

EAP-AKA for Secure Access to WLAN

EAP-AKA [1] is an EAP protocol for authentication, and session key generation using the AKA mechanism based on the USIM card in the I-WLAN access network. This allows USIM-based authentication and key agreement between an MN and a non-3GPP technology access network such as Wi-Fi. The EAP contains a negotiation procedure where the authenticator (such as AP) requests information about which authentication method would be used. The EAP server is located on a backend authentication server using an AAA protocol.

The process of secure access to I-WLAN based on EAP-AKA authentication mechanism is similar to secure access to 3G network that involves three phases. Here we only focus on the second phase authentication and key agreement. In EAP-AKA, after MN authenticates AS successfully, the USIM in MN calculates keys CK and IK, which will subsequently be used to derive the EAP master key (MK). Then, after AS authenticates MN, the MN and AP will respectively derive important security keys, such as the master session key (MSK), which will be used to generate a new transient session key TSK for secure communication. A new MSK can be derived from the MK upon handover or when the MSK lifetime is exceeded, and the TSK is generated by a four-way handshake process.

Generally, after the successful mutual authentication between MN and AS, the MN and the AP will have a four-handshake using the common MSK to generate session keys. Now, the secure access to I-WLAN is established by the secure communication between MN and AP.

4.3.2.4   Unified Authentication System for SHAWK Platform

Design of Unified Authentication System

In order to achieve secure access on **SHAWK** platform, we constructed an open platform based on AAA solution and IEEE 802.1X port-based access control mechanism, which includes supplication, authenticator and authentication server. We also implement several industrial authentication mechanisms, such as EAP-TTLS and EAP-PEAP.

For authentication in the 3G-WLAN integrated network, there is one major technical challenge that needs to be tackled. It is how to design a 3G HLR/AuC for unified authentication, as we are not allowed to modify the WSP's 3G networks. Instead, to substitute the HLR/AuC in 3G networks, we design a 3G AuC simulator, which can generate authentication vectors (AVs) based on the symmetric algorithms, and comply with the EAP-AKA protocol for secure I-WLAN access and partially with the UMTS-AKA protocol for secure 3G access. We strip the function of encryption, because the Ethernet driver cannot support the encryption algorithm Kasumi. So, we can view this as the customized UMTS-AKA authentication method. The 3G AuC also needs a corresponding authentication supplicant in the mobile equipment, which is called the USIM simulator. The USIM simulator consists of corresponding algorithms to generate AUTN, CK and IK for authentication and encryption based on the IMSI number with the shared keys. The detailed function block diagram of the unified access system is shown in Fig. 4.9.

Implementation in SHAWK Platform

We developed a unified authentication system based on the open-source software *hostapd* and *wpa_supplicant* under Ubuntu Linux 8.04 environment, and deployed it in **SHAWK** platform as shown in Fig. 4.10. The EAP-AKA authentication protocol for secure access Internet via I-WLAN and customized UMTS-AKA authentication protocol for secure access Internet via UMTS are both implemented in the system.

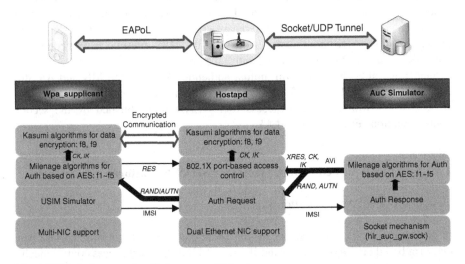

Fig. 4.9 Block diagram of unified access system

Since we did not have a 3G access network such as a base station in UMTS, we used a wired AP to substitute the access network. As for the USIM smartcard, we used a smart card reader *OMINKEY 6121* via PC/SC driver to read the IMSI number and related information. The information was configured as an authentication credential in 3G AuC simulator and USIM simulator.

Obviously, a complete 3G-WLAN unified authentication system consists of the following three parts: mobile equipment with USIM simulator, access network with wired and wireless AP, and core network with 3G AuC simulator.

Experiments and Analysis

We first conducted the experiments on the functional testing. Figure 4.11 shows a screen shot on the EAP-AKA authentication process captured by the *Wireshark* tool. The prefix with *AskeyCom* is the manufacturer's name of wireless network interface card in AP and resolved from its MAC address $00 : 11 : F5 : 50 : FC : CA$, and the prefix with *Tp-LinkT* represents the MN's network card.

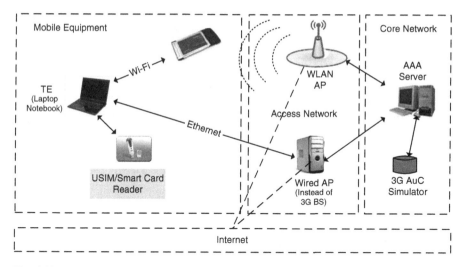

Fig. 4.10 Block diagram of unified authentication system

10 2010-06-14 16:24:12.404881	Tp-LinkT_7a:25:37	AskeyCom_50:fc:ca	ARP	192.168.18.254 is at 00:19:e0:7a:25:37
11 2010-06-14 16:24:25.934300	AskeyCom_50:fc:ca	Tp-LinkT_7a:25:37	EAP	Request, Identity [RFC3748]
12 2010-06-14 16:24:25.947293	Tp-LinkT_7a:25:37	AskeyCom_50:fc:ca	EAP	Response, Identity [RFC3748]
13 2010-06-14 16:24:25.992574	AskeyCom_50:fc:ca	Tp-LinkT_7a:25:37	EAP	Request, EAP-AKA Authentication [RFC4187]
14 2010-06-14 16:24:25.993924	Tp-LinkT_7a:25:37	AskeyCom_50:fc:ca	EAP	Response, EAP-AKA Authentication [RFC4187]
15 2010-06-14 16:24:26.002326	AskeyCom_50:fc:ca	Tp-LinkT_7a:25:37	EAP	Success
16 2010-06-14 16:24:26.002401	AskeyCom_50:fc:ca	Tp-LinkT_7a:25:37	EAPOL	Key
17 2010-06-14 16:24:26.003424	Tp-LinkT_7a:25:37	AskeyCom_50:fc:ca	EAPOL	Key
18 2010-06-14 16:24:26.004719	AskeyCom_50:fc:ca	Tp-LinkT_7a:25:37	EAPOL	Key
19 2010-06-14 16:24:26.006272	Tp-LinkT_7a:25:37	AskeyCom_50:fc:ca	EAPOL	Key
20 2010-06-14 16:24:26.014584	AskeyCom_50:fc:ca	Tp-LinkT_7a:25:37	EAPOL	Key
21 2010-06-14 16:24:26.014792	Tp-LinkT_7a:25:37	AskeyCom_50:fc:ca	EAPOL	Key
22 2010-06-14 16:24:26.025677	158.132.10.128	224.0.0.22	IGMP	V3 Membership Report / Leave group 224.0.0.251
23 2010-06-14 16:24:26.045701	0.0.0.0	255.255.255.255	DHCP	DHCP Discover - Transaction ID 0x14a57b5a

Fig. 4.11 EAP-AKA authentication procedure

It can be seen that it takes about 68 ms for authentication, 4 ms for key agreement by four-way handshake process with four interactions, and 8 ms for group-key agreement with two interactions.

In Fig. 4.12, the left part shows the successful access to I-WLAN (SSID: *wlan0*) by EAP-AKA authentication, and the right one shows successful access to virtual 3G network (network ID: *testing-aka*) by customized UMTS-AKA authentication via ethernet network card *eth0*.

We also conducted 10 group experiments with 30 times per group about the performance of authentication delay for the secure access process. Figure 4.13 shows the time of full authentication from associated state to successful authentication.

The average time of full authentication of EAP-AKA access to WLAN is about 213.8 ms. The USIM card reading and identity phases to generate supplicant identity based on PC/SC protocol occupy about 140.8 ms for 65.8 %. In the other part, the time of customized UMTS-AKA access to virtual 3G network via wired AP is an

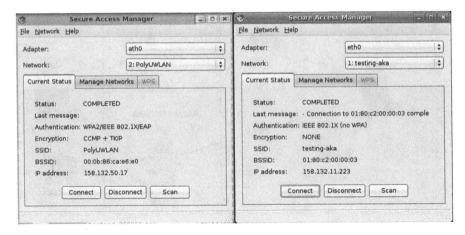

Fig. 4.12 GUI of successful unified authentication in MN

average time of 198.7 ms, which is less than the time in WLAN. It is because the
delay caused by the wired Ethernet simulates the virtual 3G secure access is much
less than wireless communication.

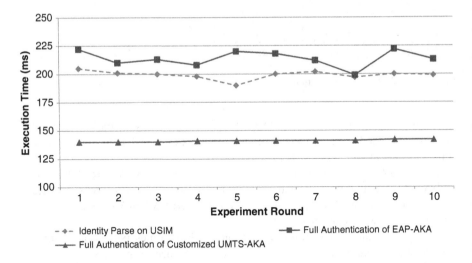

Fig. 4.13 Authentication processing time

Through the evaluation, we validated that the practical unified authentication
test-bed implemented based on 3G simulator can achieve unified secure access to
3G-WLAN interworking networks, and provide an open and effective module to
SHAWK platform.

4.3.3 VCL/VAS-Based Secure and Fast Handover

4.3.3.1 Introduction

Recently, Wi-Fi has become one of the most popular wireless access technologies worldwide, deployed widely by operators, enterprises and governments alike. Although cellular technologies such as 3G, HSPA and LTE are quickly being developed, we believe that Wi-Fi will still be very popular for the next decade because it's cheaper, easier to deploy and has higher bandwidth. Meanwhile, in the pervasive computing environment, mobile pervasive network access, especially seamless access, is crucial for many time-sensitive applications, such as real-time voice/video streaming or interactive applications.

As a competitive access technology, Wi-Fi is still not ready for mobile pervasive seamless access, because the latency of handover from one access point to another is long and not acceptable for most time sensitive applications. Apart from the long handover latency, handovers in Wi-Fi networks happen quite frequently due to the small coverage of an Wi-Fi AP and the complex deployment environments.

The Secure Handover Procedure

The whole procedure of a handover between APs executed by a mobile station (MS) contains scanning, association, authentication, configuration and location update. Scanning is to find available APs nearby, and the consuming time depends on how many channels are scanned and how much time is spent on each channel. Usually scanning can take about 100 ms. Association is for the MN to be associated with an AP and only takes several milliseconds.

Authentication is needed to ensure security between MS and AP; for home users, a pre-shared key method such as WEP or WPA-PSK is often used, and takes only a very short time. But for enterprises and operators, advanced authentication methods such as WPA/WPA2-enterprise are used to provide a higher security level. Currently, more and more enterprise-level Wi-Fi networks uses the newer WPA2, also referred to as the IEEE 802.11i standard, with stronger encryption and other advantages. However, it takes a relatively long time to complete an authentication.

IEEE 802.1X network access control is used in IEEE 802.11i, including three common entities: Supplicant (MS), Authenticator (AP), and Authentication Server (AS, a host in the network backend with the user profile, usually an AAA server using RADIUS). We omit the details of the IEEE 802.11i authentication and only briefly show how much time it costs during the roaming procedure.

As shown in Fig. 4.14, the authentication procedure includes many communication rounds among the MS, AP and AS. Typically it takes an estimated hundreds of milliseconds to finish, and even longer if the MS is roaming to a visited network (another domain different from its home domain), because the AS of the visited network needs to contact the AS of the user's home network. Configuration is the procedure of obtaining IP information, including IP address, gateway, DNS servers and configuring the air interface to gain network access on the MS. DHCP (Dynamic Host Configuration Protocol) is used by most Wi-Fi networks. The time consumed by DHCP depends on the DHCP client and server software used, and the settings on the server side, like the AP, is a DHCP server or a DHCP relay. Usually the DHCP procedure takes around hundreds of milliseconds.

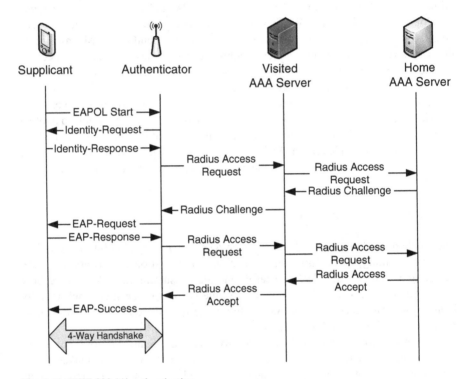

Fig. 4.14 IEEE 802.11i authentication

To support MS to move seamlessly from one AP to another, which means the application running on the MS will not be interrupted and sense the handover, a location management scheme is needed, such as Mobile IP. In this way, MS needs to register and update its location to a certain registration server like the Home Agent in the Mobile IP. The location update can be done by the MS only like the Client-side Mobile IP, or by the AP only like the Proxy Mobile IP, or both like the regular Mobile IP. The time consumed by this procedure depends on how far the MS is located from its registration server.

Reduction of the Handover Latency

There are many works optimizing the scanning procedure to reduce its effect on the handover, such as background scanning [11], in which the MS conducts channel scanning in the background during communication, instead of at the beginning of the handover; and selective scanning [14] in which the MS only scans some of the channels, etc. As for the association, nothing much can be reduced because it only takes several milliseconds.

To reduce the authentication time in IEEE 802.11i WLAN, the IEEE 802.11 working group has already defined 802.11i pre-authentication scheme, in which the client will previously authenticate with other neighboring APs through the current connected AP. Through this pre-authentication, a key called PMK (Pair-wise Master Key) is generated and held by both the MS and the pre-authenticated AP, and after the MS handovers to one of the pre-authenticated APs, it does not need to do a full authentication but just a short four-way handshake key negotiation based on the pre-generated PMK (takes about 10 ms). In this way, handover delay is significantly reduced; meanwhile, the secure level is not much sacrificed. Some of the latest open source implementations, such as *wpa_supplicant* (for the Supplicant) and *hostapd* (for the Authenticator) as well as many commercial products, already support the IEEE 802.11i pre-authentication.

Similarly to pre-authentication, pre-configuration can also be used to reduce configuration time, which means the MS previously obtains and stores the IP configuration information from the neighboring APs through the current connected AP, and uses them to configure the air interface after authentication is finished during a handover. How to reduce the location update time depends on the location management scheme used, and we will discuss it in detail in the design part of the proposed framework.

The Proposed Framework

In this work, we focus on reducing the authentication and configuration time in a practical way, which means to use and be compatible with current standards, such as IEEE 802.11i and DHCP, and modify the current software, especially software running on the network side, as little as possible.

Although the IEEE 802.11i pre-authentication can significantly reduce the authentication delay, which makes up a large part of the entire handover procedure, there are several drawbacks:

- It uses EAPOL (EAP Over LAN) frames in layer 2, which means all the protocol frames/packets are transferred and directed by MAC address, so it needs the APs to be connected in the same LAN or through bridges or a distributed system. This limits the scalability of pre-authentication. It is difficult to use them in multi-hop networks such as WMN and other IP routing based networks.

- It works only in the same domain/ESSID; cross domain operation is not supported. The reason we consider multi-domain, is because there exist many Wi-Fi networks deployed in the same area, such as in PolyU campus, where we can find over 10 different Wi-Fi networks deployed by different enterprises or Tele-operators. And end users may be able to access more than one of them, so if we can make use of multiple domains/networks, it would benefit both the end users and network owners.

To overcome the above drawbacks, we proposed a practical, secure, rapid handover (SFH) framework [6]. SFH uses the IEEE 802.11i pre-authentication and extends it to IP routing based networks and a multi-domain environment, and it also supports pre-configuration with DHCP to reduce configuration time. It is compatible with and uses current IEEE 802.11i and DHCP standards, and does not need to make modifications to current software entities on the network side, i.e. the authenticator (we use *hostapd* in the prototype implementation), DHCP server and authentication server. SFH only adds two simple standalone entities on the network side: VCL (Virtual Client) on the AP and VAS (Virtual Authentication Server) on the network backend like the same host of the AS, and corresponding software entities on the client side. Through the evaluation of the prototype of the SFH system, we validated the quality performance of the SFH framework and verify that it is able to reduce the entire handover delay. In most of the cases, the handover latency can be reduced to no more than 50 ms in an intra-domain IEEE 802.11i network, which is acceptable by most time-sensitive applications.

4.3.3.2 Design of SFH Framework

We take the IEEE 802.11i RSN pre-authentication as the example to describe why and how the SFH framework is designed, and it is quite similar to use IEEE 802.11r based on the framework.

IEEE 802.11i Pre-authentication

In the pre-authentication mode defined in IEEE 802.11i standard, as shown in Fig. 4.15, the CL (CLient/supplicant) conducts pre-authentication with the AR2 (AuthenticatoR 2, here an AR is collocated in an AP) over the connection between AR1 and AR2. The pre-authentication frames (EAPOL frames) are transmitted in the MAC layer in raw and the source and destination MAC address are the CL and AR2 correspondingly, so AR1 and AR2 in the network need to route for MAC addresses which are not for themselves, such that the pre-authentication frames can reach the right place.

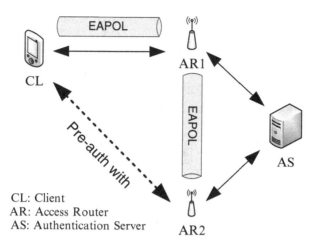

Fig. 4.15 Block diagram of IEEE 802.11i pre-authentication

Intra-domain Pre-authentication Using VCL

In order to use IEEE 802.11i pre-authentication in IP routing-based networks in the same domain, a component called VCL (Virtual Client) running on the AR is introduced.

VCL is designed to forward or route the pre-authentication frames from the CL to the target pre-authentication AR (CL to AR2 in Fig. 4.16) properly. We call it Virtual Client because it acts like a real mobile client in local from the AR2's point of view. To accomplish the proper routing, a bi-directional virtual link is created between CL and the AR2: $CL \leftrightarrow VCL1 \leftrightarrow VCL2 \leftrightarrow AR2$. Through this link, the CL can complete pre-authentication with AR2 and also with other ARs correspondingly. The detailed communication flow is listed as follows.

Step 1. Request initialization

The CL starts a pre-authentication request by sending a EAPOL frame directly to AR2 with AR2's BSSID as the destination MAC address (BSSID is the same as the MAC address of the AP interface), but through the current connected AP of AR1.

Step 2. Request forwarding

After VCL1 running on AR1 captures the EAPOL frame, it will encapsulates it into a UDP packet and sends it to the corresponding VCL (VCL2 in AR2) through a UDP tunnel.

Step 3. Request processing

VCL2 receives the UDP packet, extracts the original frame and sends it to the authenticator (like *hostapd*) to cheat the authenticator that the frame is local.

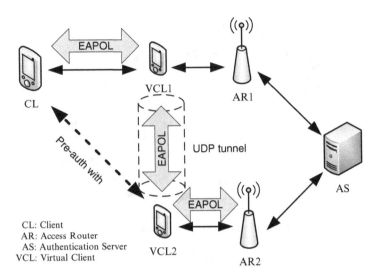

Fig. 4.16 Intra-domain pre-authentication using VCL

Step 4. Request reply

Upon receiving a pre-authentication request frame, the authenticator will generate a response frame and sends it back to the interface where it receives the request frame.

Step 5. Response forwarding

VCL2 captures the response frame, encapsulates it into a UDP packet and sends it back to VCL1 through the UDP tunnel.

Step 6. Response delivery

VCL1 receives the response UDP packet, extracts the response frame and sends it back to the CL.

Table 4.1 BSSID-VCL table

BSSID	Target VCL (UDP)
xx:xx:xx:xx:xx:xx (AR2's AP address/BSSID)	IP:Port (VCL2's UDP address)
xx:xx:xx:xx:xx:xx	IP:Port
...	...

During the above procedure, in step 2, VCL1 can obtain the destination MAC address (the BSSID of AR2) of the pre-authentication frame, but it needs to know which VCL to forward the frame to, so a BSSID-VCL table, as shown in Table 4.1, is required for VCL to find the corresponding remote VCL, according to the destination MAC address of the captured pre-authentication frame. The BSSID-VCL table can be stored locally and manually configured, or dynamically updated by querying from a central server storing all AP's information in the same domain or in a charged area of the domain.

Table 4.2 STA-VCL table

STA	Target VCL (UDP)
xx:xx:xx:xx:xx:xx (CL(STA)'s address)	IP:Port (VCL1's UDP address)
xx:xx:xx:xx:xx:xx	IP:Port
...	...

In step 5, VCL2 can obtain the destination MAC address (the MAC address of the CL) of the response frame, but it also needs to know which VCL to forward the frame to, so a STA-VCL table, as shown in Table 4.2, is needed for VCLs. The STA-VCL table is updated when VCL2 receives a request frame (encapsulated in UDP), the source MAC address of the request frame is the STA (CL)'s address, and the source address of the UDP packet is VCL1's address – it's a kind of reverse routing. Since the VCL will receive both request and response frames, we need to distinguish them so the VCL can process them properly. We define all frames from CL to AR as UP frames and all frames from AR to CL as DOWN frames. For instance, when a VCL receives a UP frame it needs to update the STA-VCL table and send it to the authenticator; when it receives a DOWN frame it only needs to send it back to the CL.

Inter-domain Pre-authentication Using VCL&VAS

If a CL wants to pre-authenticate with an AR that is not in the same domain as the current connected AR (or with different ESSID), the above VCL method cannot help, because the target VCL belongs to another domain and might be behind some gateway, making it unable to be communicated with directly. Also, it may not be allowed that the inner ARs can directly communicate with nodes from outside of the domain. Like the proxy server of the RADIUS system, we introduce the Virtual Authentication Server (VAS), which is designed to forward pre-authentication frames between domains.

As showed in Fig. 4.17, to accomplish the proper inter-domain routing, a bi-directional virtual link between CL and AR2 is created: $CL \leftrightarrow VCL1 \leftrightarrow VAS1 \leftrightarrow VAS2 \leftrightarrow VCL2 \leftrightarrow AR2$. The detailed procedure is listed as follows.

Step 1. Request initialization
   The CL starts a pre-authentication request frame (an UP frame) to AR2 through AR1.
Step 2. Request forwarding
   VCL1 captures the UP frame, checks the destination MAC address and finds the frame is to another domain (ESSID), VCL1 encapsulates the frame and sends it to VAS1 of domain1 through UDP tunnel. Since it's not feasible and practical that VAS can route the frame to the right VAS according to the BSSID (otherwise the VAS needs to know all BSSIDs of all domains with a roaming agreement), VCL1 will add the ESSID information of the BSSID into the UDP packet for the VAS.

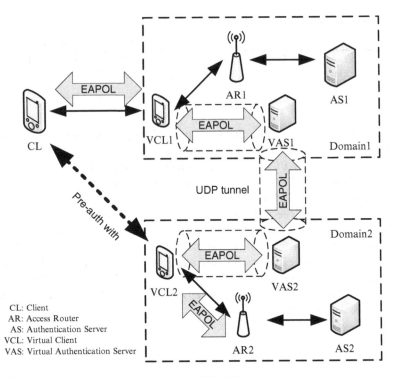

Fig. 4.17 Inter-domain pre-authentication using VCL&VAS

Step 3. STA-VCL table update at current domain

VAS1 receives the UP frame and checks the pre-configured ESSID-VCL table, as shown in Table 4.3, in which VCL and VAS are equivalent as an address in tables. All the information in the table is filled according to the roaming agreements of the current domain with other domains. Then, VAS1 determines the target VAS (VAS2) address according to the attached ESSID information, re-encapsulates the frame, and then sends it to VAS2. Meanwhile, VAS1 will update the STA-VCL table according to the source MAC address (the CL's MAC address) of the frame, so that it can route the corresponding DOWN frame to the right VCL.

Step 4. STA-VCL table update at target domain

VAS2 receives the UP frame, also updates the STA-VCL table (actually a VAS address) according to the source MAC address of the frame, determines the target VCL address (VCL2) according to the destination MAC address from the BSSID-VCL table, and sends the UP frame to VCL2 through the UDP tunnel.

Step 5. STA-VCL table update at target VCL

VCL2 receives the UP frame, updates the STA-VCL table accordingly, and sends it to the authenticator (AR2).

Step 6. Request reply

AR2 receives the UP frame, generates a DOWN frame and sends it back to the interface where it receives the UP frame.

Step 7. Response forwarding

Upon capturing or receiving the DOWN frame, VCL2, VAS2 and VAS1 accordingly determine the target VCL/VAS from the STA-VCL table, according to the destination MAC address of the frame, and send it to the matched VCL/VAS through the UDP tunnel.

Step 8. Response delivery

VCL1 receives the DOWN frame and sends it back to the CL.

Table 4.3 ESSID-VCL table

ESSID	Target VCL/VAS (UDP)
SFH-Test1	IP:Port
SFH-Test2	IP:Port
...	...

In step 4, VAS needs to have all APs information in the BSSID-VCL table in the same domain or in a charged area of the domain, which means the VAS can be the central server having the global BSSID-VCL information and VCLs can query from it. And there is an issue in step 2, which is how the VCL1 knows the ESSID of the target BSSID, which can be solved by: (a) CL helps the VCL by sending the ESSID-BSSID mapping information to the VCL; (b) VCL scans the neighboring APs and obtains the ESSID-BSSID information itself. But the second method might not work all the time, because neighboring APs might not all be visible to the AP. So we took the first method and let the CL send a BSSID-ESSID information update to the VCL of the current connected AR every time it retrieves a new scan result.

Pre-configuration

Similar to the pre-authentication procedure, if the CL obtains the IP configuration information (called lease for DHCP) from the neighboring APs through the current connect AP, and configures the interface using pre-fetched information as soon as it finishes the authentication during a handover, then the CL configuration time can be reduced to a very small value, such as several milliseconds. This pre-configuration (here we only consider DHCP) scheme is quite similar to the pre-authentication scheme, so it may also use the VCL/VAS system to forward the DHCP messages.

The problem, is that DHCP uses UDP to communicate, but the VCL/VAS routes frames according to MAC addresses, so the standard DHCP cannot use VCL/VAS directly. Fortunately, we found that although the DHCP messages are UDP packets, the communication still relies on MAC address: the DHCP request (from client to server, can also be classified as UP frames) uses broadcast MAC address (e.g. $FF:FF:FF:FF:FF:FF$) and the DHCP response (from server to client, can also be classified as DOWN frames) have to specify the client's MAC address as the destination address. It is because that the client has no any IP address yet before it gets configured by DHCP server (the source MAC address of a DHCP message is the corresponding sender's address). So, the MAC address of the destination in the DHCP request packets is required to be revised to the MAC address of the target AP (the AP from which the client wants to obtain configuration information). After that, both DHCP request and response packets can be routed by the VCL/VAS system.

The VCLs also needs to **cheat** the DHCP server or relay running on the AP by sending the DHCP request to them, capturing the DHCP response from them, and then sending it back to the client.

Reuse PMKs and DHCP Leases

After a CL authenticates or pre-authenticates with an AS through an AR, both the CL and AR will hold the same PMK, which is used for the CL and AR to do mutual authentication and negotiate keys for data encryption. The PMK for one pair of CL and AR has a lifetime, which is usually hours, and the default value of $wpa\_supplicant$ / $hostapd$ is 24 h, and before the PMK lifetime expires, the CL is able to authenticate with the AR using this cached PMK instead of generating a new one through another full authentication with the AS.

Similarly, the DHCP configuration information called lease also has a lifetime, which depends on the settings of the DHCP server (usually several hours or even longer), and before the lifetime of a lease obtained from an AP expires, the CL can still use the lease to configure the interface when it connects to the same AP, because the DHCP server still reserves the lease for the CL and other CLs cannot use it.

So, by reusing the PMK and lease for every AP, we can reduce the traffic overhead introduced by pre-authentication and pre-configuration to the network. Usually, several hours is quite long enough for users to finish a session of a certain application.

4.3.3.3   Implementation Details

The Prototype

We have implemented a prototype of the VCL/VAS system supporting IEEE 802.11i RSN pre-authentication and DHCP pre-configuration, together with a pre-configuration agent on the mobile client. All of the software entities, including VCL, VAS and PCA, are implemented using C code, and have been compiled and tested under Linux on x86-based computers. We used several well-known toolkits to set up the software environments, including $wpa\_supplicant$ as the supplicant on the client side and $hostapd$ as the authenticator on the AP and $freeradius$ as the RADIUS server.

Pre-authentication

As shown in Fig. 4.18, pre-authentication is between the Supplicant (mobile client) and the Target Authenticator (AP). The VCL/VAS system routes forwards their messages to the corresponding destinations, and is transparent to them, which means both Supplicant and Target Authenticator see each other in a local area, such as a LAN.

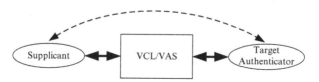

Fig. 4.18 Pre-authentication using VCL/VAS

The message flow of pre-authentication is as described in Sects. 2.2 and 2.3. We use the *wpa_supplicant* as the Supplicant on the client side, because it supports IEEE 802.11i pre-authentication and is open source, so the original UP pre-authentication frames are generated and the DOWN pre-authentication frames are processed by *wpa_supplicant*. On the other hand, *hostapd*, which is developed by the same organization as the *wpa_supplicant*, is used as the Authenticator and generates the original DOWN pre-authentication frames and process UP pre-authentication frames.

To obtain the original UP pre-authentication frames generated by *wpa_supplicant*, we use the open source *libpcap* to capture MAC frames, and the IEEE 802.11i RSN pre-authentication protocol has been assigned a unique 16-bit field type number (0x88C7) called EtherType, which is used to indicate which protocol is encapsulated in the payload of an Ethernet Frame, so it's easy to capture UP pre-authentication frames on the AP by setting up a simple filtering rule. After receiving a DOWN pre-authentication frame, the VCL directly injects the frame into the AP's interface also using the *libpcap*, and the *wpa_supplicant* will receive it at the client side. In order to interact with the Authenticator (*hostapd*), we create a virtual Ethernet device on the AP by using the TUN virtual network kernel driver in Linux, and configure the *hostapd* to receive and send pre-authentication frames through the virtual device; and the VCL on the AP, which creates the virtual device, can read and write frames from it.

The *wpa_supplicant* generates and processes the pre-authentication frames, and stores all generated PMKs paired with APs. We can use control interfaces provided by it to control which AP it should pre-authenticate, and check whether an AP has been pre-authenticated, and the lifetime of PMKs for the APs. An entity called Pre-Authentication Agent (PAA) is introduced to do this job. The *wpa_supplicant* also has its own logic to control when and which AP to pre-authenticate (pre-authenticate with all available neighboring APs with the same ESSID/domain). It can only support APs with the same ESSID, so we need to modify the *wpa_supplicant* to eliminate its own pre-authentication logic, and make it support multi-ESSID/domain. By doing this, the Handover Manager on the client can fully control when and which AP to pre-authenticate.

Pre-configuration

As shown in Fig. 4.19, the Pre-Conf Agent (Pre-Configuration Agent) on the client gets the IP configuration information (DHCP leases) from the target DHCP server on the target AP by using a standard DHCP protocol through the VCL/VAS system. The VCL/VAS system is transparent to the DHCP server in order to avoid modifying the standard server implementation, but the DHCP client needs to be re-designed and developed, because it needs to get DHCP leases from multiple servers, manage multiple leases (i.e. lifetime) and configure the interface using one of the leases. At the beginning, we want to use the standard DHCP packets, which are DHCP discovery and DHCP request messages sent by the client, for the PCA, and only change the destination MAC address to the address of the target AP.

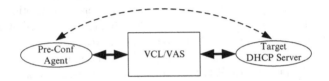

Fig. 4.19 Pre-configuration using VCL/VAS

However, we found the DHCP server on the current AP (we've tested ISC DHCP server and udhcpd) will also accept messages sent by the PCA, no matter what the destination MAC address is, and will send out DHCP response messages. This will generate much useless traffic and waste the lease resource of the DHCP server, so we need to distinguish the pre-configuration messages from normal DHCP messages. As with pre-authentication, we borrow an unused 16-bit EtherType number 0x8B00 from the public list of IEEE 802.3 website (13) and assign it as the signature of pre-DHCP packets.

The PCA generates DHCP messages (DHCP discovery and DHCP request), which we also call pre-DHCP UP frames, with changes in the destination MAC address to the target AP's address and the EtherType field to 0x8B00. The pre-DHCP UP frames will be captured by the VCL (VCL1) running on the current AP, and forward them to the target VCL (VCL2) through the VCL/VAS system according to the destination MAC address. Upon receiving a pre-DHCP UP frame, the VCL2 will change its EtherType value back to IP 0x0800, and inject it to the physical interface, which is listening by the DHCP server. The DHCP server processes the messages and generates responses, and the VCL2 needs to capture those DHCP responses from the DHCP server, and send them (pre-DHCP DWON frames) back to VCL1 according to the destination MAC address of the response packets, and further, the PCA on the client can receive them from the air sent by VCL1. Here the DHCP responses received by the PCA are also with EtherType 0x8B00, and this change can be done either by VCL1 or VCL2 (in the prototype we choose to change it on the VCL2 – the server side).

For the local DHCP requirement, i.e. the first time the client connects to a network, or the lifetime of the pre-fetched lease of the just connected AP expires, it can be done by any standard DHCP client. However, we also use the PCA to handle the local DHCP requirement, because the local AP may become the future neighboring AP, and the client may come back and reuse the lease before it expires. We treat the local DHCP packets in the same way as the pre-DHCP packets, which means they both use EtherType 0x8B00, and can be handled by the VCL/VAS system, except the target VCL will be the current VCL itself for the local DHCP packets. By doing this, both the PCA and the VCL don't need to know whether a packet/frame is local or not – they simply do the same process.

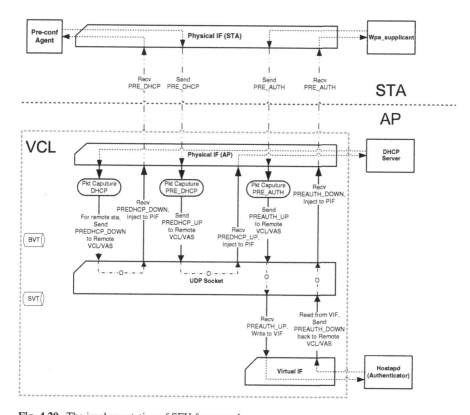

Fig. 4.20   The implementation of SFH framework

Figure 4.20 demonstrates the message/frame flow of the entire SFH framework (except for the VAS part, because the VAS simply routes messages according to the routing tables) and where and how they are transmitted, received and handled (the arrows through the UDP socket with a small circle in the middle mean the message/frame is forwarded to another corresponding VCL by UDP).

4.3.3.4   Experimentation and Evaluation

In this part, we evaluated the handover performance of the SFH framework. As a typical pro-authentication solution, our SFH framework mainly reduces the authentication time and IP configuration time during the entire handover procedure. In the following evaluation, we will take authentication delay and configuration delay as two major metrics to quantify the handover performance. We set up a mini-testbed based on **SHAWK** platform, which consisted of two administrative domains and one mobile node. The detailed configuration of the testing scenario is listed as follows.

- Supplicant: A notebook with a TP-LINK TL-WN610G PCMCIA IEEE 802.11 b/g card (based on Atheros chipsets) using $madwifi$ driver 0.9.4, running Ubuntu Linux 9.04, modified $wpa\_supplicant$ 0.6.9 and the Pre-Conf Agent daemon.
- Authenticator: Two T902 Mesh Routers with 3 mini-PCI a/b/g wireless interface cards (2 for mesh backbone and 1 for client access), running customized Linux, $hostapd$ 0.6.9, the ISC DHCP server 3.1.3, and the VCL daemon.
- Authentication Server: Two computers respectively for two administrative domains, running Ubuntu Linux 9.04, $freeradius$ 2.1.0 and the VAS daemon.

The total handover delay is divided into three main part, including *Authentication* delay, *Configuration* delay and *Switching* delay. The *Authentication* delay and *Configuration* delay are correspondingly defined as the time caused by pre-authentication phase and pre-configuration phase in the SFH framework. In the entire evaluation period, we recorded all the entry and exit time for total handover, pre-authentication and pre-configuration.

The experimental results based on ten times of measurements are plotted in Fig. 4.21. From the curve for *Configuration* time in the above figure, the *Configuration* time is a little longer than expected. It is because that there is some delay from the time for completion of configuration to the time when the configuration is actually taken effect in the physical interface. After parameter tuning in Linux system, this delay can be further reduced to improve fast handover.

In average, the segmented time for authentication is 8.8 ms, configuration is 6.9 ms and total handover is 16.9 ms. Through the evaluation, we validated the SFH framework, which extends the original IEEE 802.11i pre-authentication to multi-hop IP routing based networks and inter-domain environments, and supports pre-configuration.

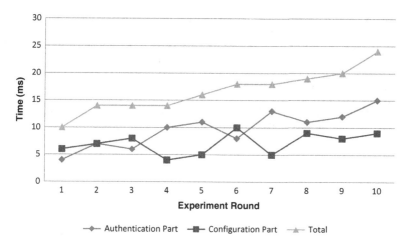

Fig. 4.21 Total handover latency and its decomposition

References

1. 3GPP: Ts 133 234 v8.1.0 universal mobile telecommunications system (umts);lte;3g security;wireless local area network (wlan) interworking security (2009)
2. Aura, T., Roe, M.: Reducing reauthentication delay in wireless networks. In: Proceedings of the First International Conference on Security and Privacy for Emerging Areas in Communications Networks, SECURECOMM '05, pp. 139–148. IEEE Computer Society, Washington, DC, USA (2005). DOI 10.1109/SECURECOMM.2005.58. URL http://dx.doi.org/10.1109/SECURECOMM.2005.58
3. Braun, T., Kim, H.: Efficient authentication and authorization of mobile users based on peer-to-peer network mechanisms. In: Proceedings of the Proceedings of the 38th Annual Hawaii International Conference on System Sciences – Volume 09, HICSS '05, pp. 306.2–. IEEE Computer Society, Washington, DC, USA (2005). DOI 10.1109/HICSS.2005.226. URL http://dx.doi.org/10.1109/HICSS.2005.226
4. Cao, J., Zhang, C., Zhang, J., Deng, Y., Xiao, X., Xiong, M., Zhou, J., Zou, Y., Yao, G., Feng, W., Yang, L., Yu, Y.: Shawk: Platform for secure integration of heterogeneous advanced wireless networks. In: AINA Workshops, pp. 13–18 (2012)
5. Deng, Y., Wang, G., Cao, J.: Practical unified authentication for 3g-wlan interworking. Journal of Information & Computational Science 9: 7 9(7), 1–9 (2012)
6. Deng, Y., Wang, G., Cao, J., Xiao, X.: Practical secure and fast handoff framework for pervasive wi-fi access. Information Security, IET 7(1), 22–29 (2013). DOI 10.1049/iet-ifs.2012.0092
7. Georgiades, M., Akhtar, N., Politis, C., Tafazolli, R.: Aaa context transfer for seamless and secure multimedia services over all-ip infrastructures. In: Fifth European Wireless Conference – Mobile and Wireless Systems beyond 3G. Barcelona, Spain (2004)
8. IEEE: Rfc 3374 – problem description: Reasons for performing context transfers between nodes in an ip access network (2002). URL http://www.ietf.org/rfc/rfc3374.txt
9. IRTF, I.R.T.F.: Rfc 6252: A framework of media-independent pre-authentication (mpa) for inter-domain handover optimization (2011). URL http://tools.ietf.org/html/rfc6252
10. Kwon, H., Cheon, K., Roh, K., Park, A.: Usim based authentication test-bed for umts-wlan handover. In: Proc. of INFOCOM'06, Poster and Demo Session. Citeseer, Barcelona, Spain (2006)

11. Saxena, N., Roy, A.: Novel framework for proactive handover with seamless multimedia over wlans. Communications, IET **5**(9), 1204–1212 (2011). DOI 10.1049/iet-com.2010.0004
12. Tews, E., Beck, M.: Practical attacks against wep and wpa. In: Proceedings of the second ACM conference on Wireless network security, WiSec '09, pp. 79–86. ACM, New York, NY, USA (2009). DOI 10.1145/1514274.1514286. URL http://doi.acm.org/10.1145/1514274.1514286
13. Wikipedia: Wired equivalent privacy (2012).   URL http://en.wikipedia.org/wiki/Wired_ Equivalent_Privacy#Flaws
14. Yao, G., Cao, J., Yan, Y., Ji, Y.: Secured fast handoff in 802.11-based wireless mesh networks for pervasive internet access. IEICE Transactions **93-D**(3), 411–420 (2010)

Chapter 5
Summary

With the title *Seamless and Secure Communications over Heterogeneous Wireless Networks*, this book provides an overview of the requirements, challenges, design issues, and major techniques for seamless and secure communications over heterogeneous wireless networks. It presents the latest results from related research and project works for handover management, mobility management, security-enabled roaming to support seamless and secure communications. In addition to studying the latest seamless and secure roaming techniques, we also share our own experiences in implementing such techniques over heterogeneous wireless networks based on past research projects, thus shortening the gap between theoretical results and actual practice.

With increasing demands for mobile computing and mobile commerce in modern society, there is a long future ahead for the heterogeneous wireless network environment. The importance of mobility management in such a network will be much clearer from the process of network convergence, business integration and terminal diversity. We hope it will provide important implications for guiding 4G research, and for the future of mobility management techniques.

J. Cao and C. Zhang, *Seamless and Secure Communications over Heterogeneous Wireless Networks*, SpringerBriefs in Computer Science, DOI 10.1007/978-1-4939-0416-7_5, © The Author(s) 2014

Index

J. Cao and C. Zhang, *Seamless and Secure Communications over Heterogeneous Wireless Networks*, SpringerBriefs in Computer Science, DOI 10.1007/978-1-4939-0416-7,
© The Author(s) 2014